JUNCTION AVENUE THEATRE COMPANY

MALCOLM PURKEY and PIPPA STEIN

WITWATERSRAND UNIVERSITY PRESS

'Sophiatown' was first performed at the Market Theatre, Johannesburg, on 19 February 1986, with the following cast:

JAKES:	Patrick Shai
MINGUS:	Arthur Molepo
MR FAHFEE:	Ramolao Makhene
LULU:	Doreen Mazibuko
MAMARITI:	Gladys Mothlale
PRINCESS:	Madidi Maphoto
RUTH:	Minky Schlesinger
CHARLIE:	Siphiwe Khumalo

The play was created in workshops by: Angus Gibson, Ruth Jacobson, Liz Johannson, William Kentridge, Siphiwe Khumalo, Doreen Mazibuko, Arthur Molepo, Gladys Mothlale, Ramolao Makhene, Malcolm Purkey, Sarah Roberts, Minky Schlesinger, Tessa Spargo, Pippa Stein

Additional material was provided by: Jane Dakile, Deborah James, Madidi Maphoto, Colin Purkey and Patrick Shai

Directed by Malcolm Purkey

Designed by Sarah Roberts and William Kentridge

Lighting design by Gerry Coughlan

Choreography by Jill Waterman

The play was produced in association with the Market Theatre Company

We thank very sincerely the following people who provided us with invaluable information, allowing the company to interview them at length: Jane Dakile, Don Mattera, Nadine Gordimer, Es'kia Mphahlele, Baruch Hirson, Theo Mthembu, Father Trevor Huddleston, Anthony Sampson, Kort Boy, Phillip Stein and Arthur Maimane

Sophiatown (the play) copyright 1986

This play is strictly protected by copyright. Any requests for performing rights should be made to:
JUNCTION AVENUE THEATRE COMPANY
c/o 21 Liddle Street, Bertrams 2094

First published in 1988 by David Philip Publisher (Pty) Ltd.
Published in 1993 by Witwatersrand University Press

ISBN 1 86814 236 1

© 1988 (the book of the play) Junction Avenue Theatre Company
All rights reserved
PRINTED BY CLYSON PRINTERS (PTY) LTD, MAITLAND

CONTENTS

Sophiatown – The Place   iv

'Sophiatown' – The Play   xi

Act One   1

Act Two   48

Act Three   77

Sophiatown – The Place

We called it Kofifi. We didn't want to use that word of Sophia. We just wanted our own name.[1]

– George 'Kort Boy' Mbanlweni
one-time leader of the American Gang

* * *

Finally, it was about people living together, robbing each other, killing each other, giving birth to others and creating ordinarily a society that one would find in America, perhaps in Canada, where a new frontier was being raised; Sophiatown was that, it was preparing the people for a new frontier. And then it was just wiped out.[2]

– Don Mattera, poet, journalist and former gangster

In 1897 an investor named Herman Tobiansky bought 237 acres of land four and a half miles (about seven kilometres) west of Johannesburg intending to develop an attractive white suburb on the site. He named the suburb after his wife, Sophia and the streets after his children. The Johannesburg Town Council, however, successfully destroyed Tobiansky's dream when they decided to build sewerage disposal facilities in an area next to the township and whites lost interest in buying property there.

Though the Sophiatown Tobiansky had dreamed of was not to be, in its place grew another Sophiatown – a colourful, vibrant, violent and sometimes sordid place that was to become both a name linked with a flourishing period of creativity in writing, music and politics, and a powerful metaphor for the destruction brought about by the Nationalist Government's policy of 'separate development'.

The Council itself began to develop property to the west of Johannesburg. Its first move was to build a new municipal location for three thousand families which was called Western Native Township. Now Tobiansky's Sophiatown was surrounded by a 'non-European' area and Tobiansky began to sell plots in the township to blacks, coloureds and Indians.

* * *

What made Sophiatown so special was the freedom of spirit amongst the people who lived there. They didn't feel constrained by any boundaries and it showed in their easy-going lifestyle. There was a great mixture of people passing through because of the freedom of mobility. One never had a sense of being cramped. It was a place where people could express themselves more freely than in any other place. Sophiatown had structures, it was never a shanty town. It was a real suburb with front gates which said, 'This is how I like to live.'[3]

– Es'kia Mphahlele, writer and lecturer

It was to become one of the few areas in the country in which Africans were allowed to own property and in which anybody who could afford it, regardless of their race, could own a business.

There was no fence around the township as there was around other black municipal locations. There was no superintendent and nobody had to get permission to live there.

The population of Sophiatown grew rapidly from the early 1920s with people of all shades and income groups moving in and building homes or occupying the shacks and rooms and huts which proliferated in the backyards of homeowners who needed to augment their incomes by collecting rent. In the 1930s the population of Sophiatown was increased by the arrival of thousands of workers who were primarily tenants. In fact, property owners made up only 2 per cent of the population whereas tenants accounted for 82 per cent and sub-tenants 16 per cent.[4]

Relationships between property owners and tenants were often strained. Rack-renting became widespread and overcrowding became more and more of a problem as the number of built-up stands increased by more than 300 per cent between 1937 and 1950. At one time Sophiatown was estimated to be home to about 130 000 people.[5]

Among the causes of the friction between landlords and their tenants were late payment of rent which upset the owners and the lack of access to water which affected the quality of life of the tenants. Property owners had to pay high water rates so many of them restricted the quantities of water used by their tenants by locking taps between 9am and 4pm and again from 8pm.

In addition, facilities were limited and yards with only one toilet or tap, or none at all, were often shared by several families.

Despite the strains, though, there are many who remember Sophiatown with affection as a real home and a real community with a personality all of its own.

* * *

> *I think that the most important thing about Sophiatown was the tremendously vital community which had to battle for any kind of dignity, so it was very alive. Of course it was a very violent place.*[6]
> – Father Trevor Huddleston, Anglican priest

Crime and violence were a characteristic of the area which became known as the Chicago of South Africa as gangs like The Americans, The Russians, The Berliners, terrorised residents and, sometimes, each other.

One well-known resident, Dr Nthato Motlana, described the youth gangs as 'out and out killers ... Sophiatown had been turned into the killing fields of Vietnam. I mean they just killed. It was dangerous living in Sophiatown.'[7]

Gang violence against Sophiatown residents escalated. The gangs operated mainly from the city bus terminus in Diagonal Street which was used by Sophiatown commuters. In 1951, after the District Commandant of Police turned down a request by residents that a commission of inquiry be set up to investigate the problem, a Sophiatown property owner, a Mr Lethoba, founded in 1951 a civil guard, its members known as *'bangalalas'*.

The move, however, proved to be a mixed blessing and soon the guards were being accused of 'legalised hooliganism'.

* * *

> *...it was very much like a scene from Falstaff – a funny mixture of people with the odd pickpocket in the background. It was wildly romantic and enormously good company. The talk was tremendously entertaining partly because of the explosive African style but it was often very well read, an odd mixture of academic knowledge with drunken conversation.*[8]
> – Anthony Sampson, former Editor of *Drum*

Violent it may have been, squalid, overcrowded and with its full share of social problems, but Sophiatown was something else as well. It was, in the 1950s, the centre of much of the country's intellectual activity, a multiracial wellspring within whose shebeens leading journalists, writers, musicians and politicians exchanged ideas and nurtured their creativity.

Linked always with its name are the names of writers like Es'kia Mphahlele, Henry Nxumalo, Can Themba, Nat Nakasa, Bloke Modisane, Lewis Nkosi and Don Mattera. Here Todd Matshikiza would commandeer any available piano and play all night and Kiepie Moeketsi would blow his saxophone 'until he fell over'.[9] It was in the shebeens of Sophiatown that Dolly Rathebe and Miriam Makeba exercised their remarkable voices. 'Whenever anything went on there was somebody there playing ... it's interesting how the music spread because the mixing spread,' comments writer Nadine Gordimer.[10] It was, she recalls, 'a time of tremendous, memorable parties.'[11]

Still, the partying and the lively culture – American jazz, the birth of the Kwela, evenings in the Odin cinema – were only a small element of life in the township. Sophiatown, observes Es'kia Mphahlele, 'was, on the whole, not that "Bohemian". The "Bohemian" side of it was the gloss. The Bohemians could be counted as a class, those people who had had an education and felt somehow that there was a kind of lawlessness about African life generally. They felt, "What is the use of trying to live within the law?" so rather than break the law, they would act "Bohemian" and go against social custom and privilege.'[12]

* * *

> *For us, who are former residents of Sophiatown, it is important that we write the story of the township, so that coming generations should not be given distorted history about the resistance of their people ... We want the younger generations to know of the sacrifices and sufferings of men, women, and children who woke up one morning to find the township looking like a place under siege.*[13]
> – Maggie Resha, ANC supporter and Sophiatown resident

In 1948 the National Party came to power and soon established the policy of apartheid with its Group Areas Act and its Resettlement Act which were aimed at preventing people of different races from living together and it was not long before Sophiatown was declared a 'Black Spot' and was scheduled for removal.

All black residents, the government decreed, were to be resettled in three townships in Soweto – Meadowlands, Dube and Diepkloof. The coloured, Indian and Chinese members of the community too would have to move to their own 'group areas'.

The government created a Resettlement Board whose task it was to conduct the removal. Members of the Board went from house to house, collecting the names of members of each family and instructing landlords to sell their properties to the government.

But the property owners of Sophiatown were not going to take their eviction lying down and, as part of an organised campaign of resistance, deliberately made things difficult for the Board by giving wrong names and inaccurate numbers of people in the houses. The result was that it took two years for the Board to collect all the names.

At a meeting on 5 October 1952 the property owners, who had constituted themselves as the African Anti-Expropriation Ratepayers Association (AAERA), met to respond to a letter addressed to them by the 'Ad Hoc Committee appointed by the Minister of Native Affairs to implement the Western Areas Scheme'. They insisted on being recognised as Johannesburg ratepayers.

At the centre of the Association's objection was the issue of the loss of freehold rights. The property owners believed the compensation they were offered would give them 'little or no scope for investment, at any event not in land because all limited areas where land could be bought were under the threat of expropriation and removals'.[14]

Many who were too old or incapacitated to work had put all their savings into properties from which they received rent. In Meadowlands they would not be allowed to rent because the township was laid out on a 'one-man-one-plot' basis.

The problem for Sophiatown's property owners was that in order to be able to put up any significant resistance to removal, they were dependent on support from their tenants, an unlikely scenario in view of the strained relationships in many cases, caused by years of exploitation of tenants.

So, in the battle for Sophiatown, resistance passed from the control of the property owners into that of the Transvaal branch of the African National Congress (ANC) and the Transvaal Indian Congress (TIC). The National Executive Committee of the ANC took the campaign over in April 1954.[15]

From the time the first threat of removal was made in 1953, the ANC had begun to mobilise residents, calling for tenants and landlords to unite against the removal.

The slogan of the campaign, which appeared on walls all over the township was *Asihambi. Ons dak nie* (We Won't Go). A Freedom Song was composed: *'Sophiatown likaya lam asihambi'* (Sophiatown is my home; we are not going) were the words, sung to the tune of a well-known hymn, the same tune used today with the words *Senzeni na* (What have we done?).

* * *

> *There was this tremendous shock when the police just came in and started moving people, just like that. To me it seemed the end of a certain set of multiracial assumptions.*[16]
> – Anthony Sampson

Late in January 1955 the government announced that the date of the removal would be 12 February. A huge protest meeting was held on Freedom Square (the site of many memorable political meetings).

Maggie Resha remembers that 'The shock and anger of the people that day was evidenced by cries, at the end of each speech, of "We want arms to face the Boers". The crowd was so big that the square was overflowing with people; some were on top of the roofs of houses near the square, others were in trees. The voices which called for arms mostly came from the edges of the meeting. Youth Leaguers and Volunteers usually stood there to control the crowds and also to guard people and to see that they did not lose their tempers if they were provoked by the SB (Special Branch) and the police.'[17]

The residents established the Western Areas Protest Comittee to organise mass resistance. The ANC called for five thousand Freedom Volunteers to mobilise the people around the slogan of defiance *'Asihambi'*. A non-violent stayaway was planned for 12 February 1955, the day the removals were due to start.

* * *

> *Before we had even opened the front door, I just heard the hammer on the pillar of the verandah. It so beat the pillar that it sounded like a rockfall in those mines of Carltonville, a big sound that made me wonder if I was dying. That sound went right into my heart and I shall never forget it.*[18]
> – Jane Dakile, schoolteacher

The government did not wait until the scheduled date of 12 February before it moved in on the residents of Sophiatown.

Maggie Resha recalls: 'On the evening of the 8 February, a young man came running to our house from Toby Street (the first street in Sophiatown which faced, and marked the border with the white suburb of Westdene). He told us that black policemen had been to two or three houses, telling people to pack up their belongings for removal the next day, the 9 February.'[19]

That night, Sophiatown swung into action. Volunteers were called in to move the belongings of those who had resolved to resist. Furniture and household goods were removed to empty halls and private schools in the township so, when a huge force of police arrived to move the residents of Toby Street, many of its residents had moved out. The operation succeeded in obstructing the forced removal of 50 of the 150 families who had been designated for removal on 9 February.

There were no further warnings. On 10 February – two days before the due date – two thousand police armed with sten guns, rifles and knobkerries moved into Sophiatown before dawn. People were unprepared, many had not even packed, but they were forced out of their houses, their belongings were loaded onto military lorries and taken from Sophiatown to the new location of Meadowlands. On that day, in soaking rain, 110 families were moved.

By the first day of the removals it had become apparent that the Western Areas Campaign had failed. One observer remarked: 'When the day of the removals came, the sub-tenants dumped their goods and jumped into the police and army vans singing.' Father Huddleston recalled that people were perplexed 'when the lorries moved off to Meadowlands so safely and with such apparently happy travellers'.[20]

What caused the failure of the resistance on which so many householders had placed their hopes? At least part of the reason was that there was no cohesion between property owners, tenants and sub-tenants. The property owners, through the Ratepayers Association, had emphasised that the question of freehold was a crucial element in the conflict with the government. They made no serious effort to enlist the support of their tenants and sub-tenants.

In fact, many tenants were indeed 'happy travellers'. The type of housing offered in Meadowlands appeared to be a welcome alternative to the exploitation of many of Sophiatown's landlords and the uncomfortable, overcrowded conditions in which many lived. The new houses promised space, privacy, access to water at all times and private lavatories. Most importantly, they offered security of tenure, a crucial issue. In Sophiatown many tenants had become victims of eviction not because they were rent defaulters but because other, potential tenants promised either to pay higher rents or offered property owners large sums of money to make rooms available to them.

'The arguments advanced by Congress leaders, emphasising the loss of freehold rights, made little impact on tenants and sub-tenants. For most tenants, living in single rooms under constant harassment by landlords was totally unacceptable.'[21]

Still, the resistance did produce some cohesion in the community, the strangest element of which was the involvement of the gangs. 'During the campaign against the removal,' writes Maggie Resha, 'the impossible happened. *Tsotsis* [gangsters] made a truce between themselves; they started to attend ANC meetings at Freedom Square. The atmosphere in the township changed, and people could walk at night without fear of being robbed or molested. The spirit of solidarity amongst the residents was outstanding, because the people fought against the removals as a community and the divisions of social status were buried.'[22]

* * *

> Long ago I decided to concede, to surrender to the argument that Sophiatown was a slum, after all. I am itchingly nagged by the thought that slum clearance should have nothing to do with the theft of freehold rights.[23]
> – Can Themba, journalist

The process of removals continued for five years, from 1955 to 1960 and by 1958 Sophiatown 'looked like pictures we had seen of some European cities after the last world war. It was in ruins, with the thick walls with beautiful decorations and smooth, shining steps at the entrances, all that remained to show what had been. Some people were actually squatting on pavements with their belongings; others were collecting the bricks after their houses had been demolished,' writes Maggie Resha.[24]

In the end, Sophiatown, Father Huddleston's 'violent and vital'[25] township, was razed to the ground. And in its place grew a soulless white suburb that was named ... Triomf.

Pat Schwartz

---

[1] From an interview in Pippa Stein and Ruth Jacobson (eds). 1986. *Sophiatown Speaks*, p 71. Johannesburg: Junction Avenue Press.

[2] Ibid, p 11.

[3] Ibid, p 55.

[4] Lebelo, Malesela S. 1988. Sophiatown Removals, Relocations and Political Quiescence in the Rand Townships, 1950-1965. Honours Dissertation, University of the Witwatersrand, Johannesburg.

[5] Resha, Maggie. 1991. *My Life in the Struggle: 'Mangoana O Tsoara Thipa Ka Bohaleng*, p 52. London: SA Writers, Johannesburg: Cosaw.

[6] *Sophiatown Speaks*, p 73.

[7] Sophiatown Removals, p 79.

[8] *Sophiatown Speaks*, p 43.

[9] Ibid, p 28

[10] Ibid, p 29.

[11] Ibid, p 28.

[12] Ibid, p 58.

[13] *My Life in the Struggle*, p 65.

[14] Sophiatown Removals, p 89.

[15] Ibid, p 90.

[15] *Sophiatown Speaks*, p 46.

[17] *My Life in the Struggle*, p 57.

[18] *Sophiatown Speaks*, p 6.

[19] *My Life in the Struggle*, p 58.

[20] Sophiatown Removals, p 87.

[21] Ibid, p 87.

[22] *My Life in the Struggle*, p 64.

[23] Sophiatown Removals, p 4.

[24] *My Life in the Struggle*, pp 62-3.

[25] *Sophiatown Speaks*, p 73.

'SOPHIATOWN' – THE PLAY
BY MALCOLM PURKEY

An obsession to reclaim and popularize the hidden history of struggle in our country is part of Junction Avenue Theatre Company's self-appointed task. This history has been wiped off the map by the State in its oppression of the majority of South Africans. The powerful flourishing of the contemporary theatre in South Africa, against all the odds, indicates the hunger that all South Africans have, to have their world interpreted. We need an informed and articulate new generation, steeped in the past and carefully theorizing about the future, who have shaken off the blanket of silence and are committed in the deepest way to liberation. We believe that one of the most effective ways to communicate ideas, information and feelings is through the living theatrical encounter.

When Junction Avenue Theatre Company first started in 1976, it was a group of white students, based at the University of the Witwatersrand. In this, it reflected the nature of the university at the time. Our first project, 'The Fantastical History of a Useless Man' leapt through history from 1652 to 1976, trying to evaluate the possible role of white, English-speaking South Africans in the context of the '76 Soweto uprisings. After this first project, it became very clear that a group of only white members was entirely unsatisfactory: if we were to begin to reflect the true nature of the conflicts around us, we had to become a non-racial group. Fortunately, in the theatre company Workshop '71, manifestly committed to the creation of original, progressive South African theatre, we found a powerful and challenging model. In its organization and approach to the creation of new plays, it was a working model of non-racial democracy. In 1976, when Workshop '71 dissolved, with many of its members in exile, some of its key members joined Junction Avenue Theatre Company. This gave the company the core of its current composition.

With this newly constituted group, the company explored the relationship between labour and liquor on the goldmines at

INTRODUCTION

the turn of the century in 'Randlords and Rotgut' (1978), based on an article of the same name by Charles van Onselen. This was followed by a play on the life of Breyten Breytenbach, 'Will of a Rebel' (1979) and a series of short, popular plays which toured the townships and the white suburbs: 'Dikitsheneng' (1980), which examined the complex relationship between maids and madams; and 'Security' (1979), the story of an unemployed man who is turned into a dog. Members of the company also collaborated on the creation of workers' plays with the trade union movement Ilanga Lizo Phumela Abasebenzi (1982). The urban removals in Doornfontein in the thirties and forties was the subject of 'Marabi' (1982), based on the popular novel by Modikwe Dikobe, *The Marabi Dance*.

'Marabi' was an unfinished piece of work. Dealing as it did with the State's destruction of Marabi culture and the removal by force of the black working-class from the urban areas, it provided a model for further investigation. The issue of forced removals was certainly not exhausted. The destruction of Sophiatown, an urban community of the fifties, seemed a possible next area of research. The current struggle, with its roots firmly in the Freedom Charter, had its first seeds in the momentous political events of the fifties, events which the official culture and history have attempted to hide.

Our concern to explore these issues remained an abstraction, however, until we chanced upon the following story about two well-known journalists in Jim Bailey's account of the spectacular rise of the popular fifties magazine, *Drum*:

> 'Nat [Nakasa] and Lewis [Nkosi] set up house together [in Sophiatown] and advertised for a Jewish girl to come and live with them. Despite all the legislation of South Africa, they obtained one. I met the sporting lass. She was good enough looking but very tall and thin – I could not banish the impression that she was originally constructed by being drawn through a hole, like a wire.'

What an extraordinary story! And what a spark for us! We were immediately intrigued. Who could she possibly have

INTRODUCTION

been? Why did she take up the challenge?

In the workshops, we deliberately refrained from pursuing too far the actual facts of that event, attempting rather an imaginative reconstruction. We were nonetheless aware of our enormous responsibility to the people of Sophiatown – we had to strive to remain true to the spirit of the times. And so we started a series of interviews with representative figures from the period.

We were fortunate to witness, in a workshop, four hours of the most revelatory storytelling from Don Mattera, sometime Sophiatown gangster and poet. We became awed at the scope of our task. From Mattera we learned that we had to reflect a whole network of vital subcultures, and immediately we became immersed in Tsotsitaal, an explosive articulation of street culture.

Kort Boy, leader of the American Gang, provided another challenge: how to capture the language and gesture of the rival gangs . . . how to capture the peculiar mixture of politeness and extreme violence, the obsession with dress and fancy shoes, the power of the American movies, the attitude to women . . .

Schoolteacher and Sophiatown property owner, Jane Dakile, told of the brutal destruction of her home, an unbearably moving story which set the emotional tone of the play's climax. Anthony Sampson and Nadine Gordimer, amongst others, shared their experiences of the intellectual life of Sophiatown interwoven with the pursuit of pleasure – the Softown shebeens were great meeting places for black and white bohemians.

One day we set off in four cars to Pretoria, to the film archives to study the films of the fifties, 'African Jim' and 'The Magic Garden'. There we learned of the vital importance of a particular style of music played in the Sophiatown and Johannesburg nightclubs. We also spent hours paging through *Drum* magazines from the period to establish aspects of the design style, and we read as much of the literature of the time as we could get our hands on.

As the play began to take shape, there were central

INTRODUCTION

questions to answer: what does the Jewish girl do on the first day she arrives, unannounced, into the already established Sophiatown household? Under what conditions is she accepted? How does a sixteen-year-old schoolgirl respond to the call for a school boycott in 1955, when Bantu Education is first implemented? Where does an American gangster store his goods? What was the role of a journalist from *Drum* magazine at the height of its popularity? What was the role of the resistance movement and to what extent did it affect the life of our Sophiatown household? Countless questions, researches and workshops were needed to find answers; the answers not always to be found.

One night we were exploring what happens the day Ruth arrives in Sophiatown. Suddenly Ramolao Makhene burst into our imaginary house and lauched into a tirade of words with such a powerful guiding rhythm, it was almost like an opera. 1 is for King, 2 is for Monkey, 3 is for Seawater . . . We had encountered fahfee before but never like this. A numbers system with almost mystical connotations unfolded before my eyes. This improvisation gave us the key to the key to the character that became Mr Fahfee, fahfee-runner and political activist, and opened up a whole structuring principle for the play.

Meeting at night, three times a week for six months, we attempted in the workshop to confront each other creatively across the apartheid divide. In the workshop we wished, as if by magic, to forge a collective vision of the future. Through the workshop, we found a meeting ground and a way to explore our common life experiences. One of our most important workshops centred on rites of passage: each member of the group had to enact or describe a crucial ritual[1] of transformation in his or her life. It could be private or formal.

The fascinating stories included William Kentridge's detailed description of his preparations for his Barmitzvah, how, in a cracked voice, he learned to sing parts of the Scriptures, written without vowels, in a language he didn't understand, in a flat in Hillbrow, at seven o'clock in the morning, his teacher

INTRODUCTION

refusing even to get out of bed! We listened to Siphiwe Khumalo's account of the ritual slaughter of a goat, how its bile is carefully stored, then smeared onto a motor-car's engine to protect the car from being stolen . . . What extraordinary reports for the uninitiated among us!

We spent hours in narrative workshops, examining the different structures for our story, weighing up the effects of different beginnings and endings, constantly reminding ourselves, when the seductions of a particular character's story threatened to overwhelm our story, that our central concern was to tell the story of the destruction of Sophiatown.

After six months of work, the tapes and files of recorded material became burdensomely large. I was sent off for six weeks to shape the material into a working script. After another six weeks of intensive daily rehearsal and rewriting, we were ready to open. We premiered at the Market Theatre Upstairs on 19 February 1986. The play has had many seasons since, and each season demands some kind of re-evaluation of the script. What you have before you is as close to the finished script as we are likely to get.

16 May 1988

Sophiatown

List of characters:

JAKES:	A *Drum* magazine journalist and intellectual. In his late twenties.
MINGUS:	A member of the American Gang. In his late twenties.
MR FAHFEE:	Fahfee runner and Congress activist. In his forties.
LULU:	A sixteen-year-old schoolgirl.
MAMARITI:	A Shebeen Queen and owner of a house in Sophiatown. She is the mother of MINGUS and LULU.
PRINCESS:	Lover of MINGUS and good-time girl. In her twenties.
RUTH:	A Jewish girl from the white suburb of Yeoville. In her twenties.
CHARLIE:	MINGUS's sidekick. Barely articulate. He is obsessed with shoes.

The play is set in the 1950s and takes place in MAMARITI's freehold Sophiatown house. The living area is cramped but comfortable, suggesting care and warmth. Each character, particularly, has a corner defined by his or her things. JAKES, a table, chair, typewriter, books; CHARLIE, a broken car seat and a steering-wheel; LULU, school-books, pencils and pens; MAMARITI, a comfortable armchair and a side-table covered with photographs. There are other assorted chairs and a kitchen table. There is a kitchen recess and exits to various parts of the house. The front door is located through the kitchen recess and out of sight. Three telegraph poles are placed at intervals on the set. These poles are attached to telegraph wires which run out over the audience. The action is played against a backdrop of painted images deriving from newspapers, magazines and photographs from Sophiatown and the period.

Act 1 Scene 1

(Shafts of light slowly reveal the Cast as they sing 'Kofifi Sophia'.
MINGUS *is centre stage, his hat pulled low over his eyes.)*

>Kofifi Sophia, Kofifi Sophia (2)
>Ons pola hier in Sophia (2)
>Moegoes nou moet nou gaan
>Moegoes nou moet voetsak
>Daar's nie plek vir al die G-men
>Daar's nie plek vir al die gatas
>Ons wietie met die wiebits, majietas en mataras
>Ons wietie met die wiebits, majietas en mataras
>
>(Sophiatown, Sophiatown, Sophiatown, Sophiatown (2)
>We are staying here in Sophiatown (2)
>All the stupids must move now
>All the stupids must bugger off now
>There's no place for the policemen
>There's no place for the policemen
>We're talking to the girls, the guys and the ladies)

*(*MINGUS *returns to his seat, the song quietens to a murmur and* JAKES *rises to speak.)*

JAKES: Sophiatown, Softown, Kofifi, Kasbah, Sophia . . . Place of Freedom Square, and the Back of the Moon. Place of Can Themba's House of Truth. Place of the G-men and Father Huddleston's Mission. Place of Balansky's and the Odin Cinema. And let's never forget Kort Boy and Jazz Boy and the Manhattan Brothers, and Dolly Rathebe singing her heart out – here in Sophia . . .

(The song momentarily swells.)

The Americans, the Berliners, the Gestapo, the Vultures – they fought here and blood ran in the streets of Sophia.

Can Themba, Nat Nakasa, Lewis Nkosi, Bloke Modisane wrote their best, here in Sophiatown. Tambo and Mandela walked here.

Luthuli stood, and a city's people walked past, here in Sophia.

Sophiatown, named after one Tobiansky's wife. Gerty Street, Ray Street, Edith Street, Bertha Street, named after Tobiansky's daughters. Did he know what he was making, I wonder, here in Sophia?

65 Gerty Street, that's where I found myself, in a shack at the back of a Softown cottage. Live-in at Mamariti's Diamond Shebeen. One pound a month! I say an exorbitant price to pay for a room hardly big enough to hold a bed. Tap in the yard, toilet in the corner – but it was grand because it was Softown. Freehold! It was ours! Not mine exactly, but it was ours. And it was close by to the big city – that is the why-for we wanted to stay. This! This is what made the Boere mad. I wanted to stay – they wanted me to go. Too much freedom, too much meeting, too much fantasy, too much easy access. White bohemians and black intellectuals – that meant trouble for the Boere's dream of a whites-only world.

I was banging out a living at Drum Magazine. Boxing was my beat, but I wanted to cover the Softown lifestyle. Anything could happen here, and if it did I wanted to be there. I needed stories – anything to get off the boxing beat. My brain was working overtime. I had to find something new, something different . . .

(*As* JAKES *seats himself in front of his typewriter, the song builds up again.* FAHFEE, MAMARITI, RUTH, PRINCESS *and* LULU *exit, jiving to the music. Lights change.*)

MINGUS: Jakes!

JAKES: Mingus!

MINGUS: 'n Bla van 'n man! (*Catching* CHARLIE'*s eye.*) Charlie!

JAKES: Whe've you been, Mingus? Been making trouble again?

MINGUS: Jakes, I'm in love, man. I've just been to a wonderful funeral.

JAKES: A funeral? Is there a story there?

MINGUS: Ja, skryf daar, 'I went so nobody could say I killed him.'

(CHARLIE *has crept up to* MINGUS *and begins to shine his shoes while he is still wearing them.*)

MINGUS: Hey Charlie – leave off! Leave off! Go and sleep in the car. We've a job tonight. I want you wide awake. Hey Charlie – move!

(CHARLIE *persists in trying to clean the shoes.*)

MINGUS: Go on! (MINGUS *pushes* CHARLIE *away.*) Jakes, ek wil 'n brief hê – 'n letter van love.

JAKES: A love letter for you?

MINGUS: Ja, ek's in love, met 'n real tjerrie, 'n matara, a real ding, 'n princess . . . That's her name – Princess!

JAKES: Why don't you write it yourself, Mingus? I'm working.

MINGUS: Ag man Jakes, ek kan nie skryf nie. You know that – ek kan wietie, maar ek kan nie skryf nie.

JAKES: Well, that's too bad, man. I'm busy.

MINGUS: Listen, I'll give you a story, a story for a love letter.

JAKES: A story?

MINGUS: The Americans.

JAKES: Come off it, Mingus. Everybody's got an angle on the gangsters. Mr Drum, Casey Motsitsi – everybody.

MINGUS: My personal story, Jakes. How I pull the jobs. How I met Kort Boy. How I get rid of the stuff. I'll tell you everything.

JAKES: I want names, details, the goods yards, the whole lot.

MINGUS: A story for a love letter?

JAKES: It's a deal.

MINGUS: Start writing! Write the address – I want her here tonight at six o'clock.

JAKES: Oh boy, Mingus!

4 Act 1

(CHARLIE *is trying to clean* MINGUS's *shoes again*.)

MINGUS: (*Taking off his shoes.*) Hey, Charlie, for God's sake, take them away!

(CHARLIE *retires and squats in a corner.* JAKES *types the address.*)

JAKES: How do I start?

MINGUS: Ag man, skryf man. Jy's die B.A. – intellectual. Ek is net 'n outie.

JAKES: You want me to waste my talents on a mere love letter!

MINGUS: That's your business, Jakes. Every day jy sit daar en tik-tik . . .

JAKES: Yes but that's boxing . . .

MINGUS: . . . and this is love, Jakes . . . Skryf!

JAKES: (*Typing.*) My dear darling beloved Princess! Right! The Americans.

MINGUS: Ag, skryf man, Jakes. And she must love that letter.

JAKES: First the Americans.

MINGUS: Alright! Alright! You want to know about the Americans, I'll tell you about the Americans! We want to hit the yards, the railway yards in Braamfontein, so we park the Chrysler, Charlie checks out the place. Hey Charlie, there's a guard but it's cool, it's okay. I jump out – I check for my thing, it's there. I feel for my gonee – it's there. The guard's half asleep – we throw a stone into the far corner. It's clear. We move in. We only go for the best. Jakes?

JAKES: Ja?

MINGUS: Tell her I only go for the best.

JAKES: How do you know it's the best?

MINGUS: Tell her I only go for the best.

JAKES: How do you know it's the best?

MINGUS: Easy, man – check the labels! Only genuine English

or American imports, 'Can't-gets' – Florsheims, Winthrops, Bostonians, Saxone and Manfield, Arrow shirts, suits from Simpson's, Hector Powe, Robert Hall, Dobbs, Woodrow, Borsalino hats. You tell her I'm the best dresser in town. American straights. You tell her I'm a smart guy – no messing around, and I want her here tonight at six o'clock!

JAKES: (*Typing.*) Oh boy, Mingus!

MINGUS: So we load up the cars and we're ready to go. And who the hell arrives? The Berliners – in our own territory, man! These Berliners – real bastards. Only rob the local people, man – no respect. Jakes!

JAKES: Ja?

MINGUS: Tell her I'm an honest gangster! Only rob die town, ek. So we tell them just split, man . . . Fok off! Get out, gee pad, man! Go back to Edward Road. Then this one Berliner takes out his jungle and it's war, man – Second World War all over again. Jakes!

JAKES: Ja?

MINGUS: Tell her I fought in the war, man – tell her I'm a war hero.

JAKES: You fought in the war?

MINGUS: Yes man – I fought in the planes, in the tanks, just like Clark Gable in that . . . that . . . 'Gone With the Wind'.

JAKES: I'll tell her you'll take her to the Odin Cinema.

MINGUS: Ja man! And the Ritz – for lang-arm dancing. So it's the Second World War, man. All over again. The Americans and the Berliners, but we're gonna win, man. We got the edge. I smile. I smile and move back. Jakes?

JAKES: Ja?

MINGUS: Tell her I've got a lovely smile, man. Now the thing's in my hand, man. Hey guys, gee pad, gee pad! They don't move. My thing's itching man, it's talking to me, my special Baby Brownie. Hey man, gee jy die pad, man – dis onse town. Jakes?

JAKES: Ja?

MINGUS: Tell her I own the town.

(*Enter* MR FAHFEE.)

FAHFEE: Hey, hey, hey, hey, hey! Bo Resha says the Boere own the town and we must never forget that.

JAKES: Hey Fahfee, that smells like a story.

FAHFEE: News of the Day! Dikgang tsa gompieno! Dolly Rathebe is singing in 'African Jazz and Variety' for Alf Herbert at the Windmill Theatre in Johannesburg and guess in what language she's singing?

JAKES: What?

FAHFEE: Yiddish! What's the number today, gentlemen, what's the dream?

MINGUS: Hey Fahfee – we're busy – Jake's writing me a masterpiece.

FAHFEE: Words again, Mr Jakes?

JAKES: A love letter, Fahfee.

FAHFEE: A love letter! Let me see – love . . . That's number 35 – Katpan. Or 36 – Nonkwayi. Male and female anatomicals – 35 or 36 it is!

JAKES: Love! It's just quarrels all the way.

FAHFEE: Quarrels – number 5 – the Tiger.

MINGUS: Ag man, Jakes, what do you know of love? Waar's jou ousie?

JAKES: Ek het nie.

MINGUS: Daar's die main trouble, man.

FAHFEE: So what's the love letter?

MINGUS: Read it Jakes, read it! Fahfee here is a man with an ear for numbers. Tell me this is not my number!

JAKES: It's not finished.

MINGUS: (*Threatening.*) Read it out, Jakes.

JAKES: Okay. 65 Gerty Street, Sophiatown, Johannesburg. 21st November 1954. My dear darling beloved Princess. I saw you at the funeral and I think you're smashing. I only go for the best. Winthrops, Bostonians, Simpsons, Borsalinos, and you. I'm the best dresser in town. American straights. I'm a smart guy and I don't get messed around. Be here at six o'clock tonight. I'm an honest gangster. I only go for the town centre – I don't touch Sophia. I fought in the war, in planes and tankers and I love the Odin Cinema. Balansky's is not for me – too much shouting.

MINGUS: Ja and tell her I don't like it when they piss off the balcony and throw bottles down.

JAKES: Okay, Mingus! (*Reading.*) I've got a lovely smile . . . and that's as far as we got when Mr Fahfee came in.

MINGUS: So what you think, Fahfee?

FAHFEE: Well. Is she a Diamond Lady? That's number 17. Or a Young Girl – that's number 19. I think the letter must be a romance, like: 'I spend sleepless nights dreaming of you. My heart goes put-put. I see you everywhere . . . '

MINGUS: Rubbish! It must flow like music.

FAHFEE: Alright. Alright! (*Improvising a rhythm.*) You know – you know – you know – I love you – full stop. You know – you know – you know – I want you – full stop. You know – you know – you know – I'm yours – full stop. Your most passionate American Admirer, 'Clark Mingus Gable'.

(*He concludes by miming a punctuation mark in the air.*)

MINGUS: Rubbish passionate! Jakes, just put, 'I won't wait after six!'

JAKES: Okay Mingus . . . Mr Fahfee, what's in the news today?

FAHFEE: Ah. Father Huddleston has started a Western Areas protest committee. Congress has called for five thousand volunteers. Bo Resha says, 'The time has come.'

JAKES: Did you bring those books for Lulu?

MINGUS: Politics! You leave my sister alone. She's at school and she's got a bloody lot of work. An' you, Fahfee, don't come here with your own troubles.

FAHFEE: (*Sidestepping the issues.*) Just tell me your dreams and I'll give you the right number.

JAKES: I'm dreaming up a scheme that'll floor the lot of you. Just wait – I've got a story up my sleeve that'll move me right to the top.

FAHFEE: The top? That's number 1!

JAKES: The King?

FAHFEE: Yes . . . We need help from you, Mr Drum. You must write about Sophiatown. We're not going to move, and you must tell the whole world.

JAKES: At the moment all I'm gonna tell the world about is boxing, but just you wait – promotion is just around the corner.

MINGUS: Ouens, ouens, we must finish this love letter and get it off. Charlie!

FAHFEE: So how's it gonna end?

MINGUS: How about 'Yours in loving memory'?

JAKES: That's for the dead, Mingus.

(FAHFEE *breaks into uncontrollable laughter.*)

MINGUS: Ag . . . skryf daar about die moon, man, Jakes! Charlie!

JAKES: Largely romantic. Ours is a night time love, ours is a silver light love, ours is a love as full as the moon.

FAHFEE: Your voice is like moonrays, like the silver rays it calls to me . . .

JAKES: . . . and my letter calls to you.

MINGUS: . . . to be here at six o'clock sharp! Charlie! (CHARLIE *responds*.) I want this letter to be there and back in quicker than two flaps of a dove's tail!

(*The four men break into a close harmony quartet about* PRINCESS, *love, Sophiatown, and moonlight*.)

Act 1   Scene 2

(*The scene opens with* PRINCESS *sitting on the table painting her nails*. MAMARITI *is asleep in her chair*. LULU *is preparing for school*.)

LULU: I wandered lonely as a cloud . . .
   that floats on high, above vales and hills.
   When all at once I saw a crowd,
   a host of golden daffodils.
   Besides the lakes, beneath the trees,
   fluttering and dancing in the breeze.

(*There is a knock on the door. Silence*. PRINCESS *doesn't move. Another knock*. MAMARITI *awakes with a start*.)

MAMARITI: Kom in! (*Knock*.) Kom binne! (*Knock*.) Hey kom in, come in! (*Knock*.) Jislaaik. Well if you don't want to come in, fok off man! (*She is now fully awake*.) Princess, go and open the door.

PRINCESS: I'm busy.

MAMARITI: How my son can live with you I don't know. Lulu, open the door.

LULU: I'm busy, Ma. I'm studying.

MAMARITI: For crying out loud! Stand up and go and open the door! What is going on in this house?

LULU: (*Going to the door*.) I wandered lonely as a cloud . . . (*Bangs her head*.) . . . I wandered lonesome like a cloud . . . I'll never learn this thing.

(*Enter* RUTH, *the Jewish girl from Yeoville. She is carrying two suitcases and seems prepared to move in.* LULU, PRINCESS *and* MAMARITI *draw back in surprise.*)

RUTH: Hullo! I'm Ruth. (*Silence.*) Ruth Golden. (*Silence.*) I'm the Jewish girl. (*Silence.*) I wonder if this is the right address? (*She scratches in her clutch bag.*) 65 Gerty Street?

LULU: Yes?

RUTH: Well, I came in response to the advertisement . . . Where shall I put my things?

LULU: Look, who are you?

PRINCESS: Yes, this is Sophiatown you know.

RUTH: Yes, I know. I've come in response to the advertisement.

(*Enter* MINGUS *and* CHARLIE.)

MINGUS: Hey, hey what's going on? What's happening?

LULU: This lady seems to think she's moving in.

RUTH: Yes, well . . .

MINGUS: Listen, lady, who are you and what do you want?

(CHARLIE, *who has followed* MINGUS *in, begins to paw at* RUTH's *shoes. She pretends not to notice.*)

RUTH: I'm Ruth Golden, the Jewish girl from Yeoville. I came in response to the advertisement.

(CHARLIE's *advances have become overpowering.*)

RUTH: Aaaah!

MINGUS: Charlie! Off!

LULU: Which advertisement?

RUTH: Here it is. (*She attempts to show it to* MINGUS *who stares at it, and turns away.*) 'Wanted: one Jewish girl to live in Sophiatown for study purposes. Come to 65 Gerty Street, or phone 46-7894.'

Scene 2 11

LULU: Well?

RUTH: Well, I'm Jewish.

MINGUS: So?

RUTH: So here I am . . . (CHARLIE *is at it again.*) Please!

MINGUS: Charlie, off! (CHARLIE *retreats.*) Look lady, is this some kind of a joke?

RUTH: I assure you it's not.

PRINCESS: We don't want European girls here. European girls mean trouble.

MINGUS: Where did you see this advertisement?

RUTH: In Drum Magazine.

MINGUS: Drum Magazine!

RUTH: I do read it, you know!

MINGUS: This is Jakes' business!

RUTH: Jakes!

MINGUS: Charlie! Go fetch Jakes. This is all Jakes' nonsense again. Hey look here lady, what kind of a person are you? Do you know this is Sophiatown?

RUTH: Yes! I read all about it before I came.

PRINCESS: This is a native township.

LULU: Father Huddleston says it's a freehold suburb.

(*Enter* MR FAHFEE.)

FAHFEE: Hey, hey, hey, hey, hey. News of the day! Dikgang tsa gompieno! Albert Luthuli has been banned. All houses to be sold to the Resettlement Board. (FAHFEE *turns and sees* RUTH.) O Mang?

RUTH: I beg your pardon?

FAHFEE: Wie's jy?

RUTH: Sorry?

12 Act 1

FAHFEE: Give me a number.

RUTH: What?

MINGUS: Give him a number.

RUTH: Any number?

LULU: Yes, any number.

RUTH: (*Bewildered.*) Number 17.

FAHFEE: Number 17! Diamond Lady. I knew it – that's the one for the day!

RUTH: What?

FAHFEE: 1 is for King, 2 is for Monkey, 3 is for Sea Water, 4 is for Dead Man, 5 is for Tiger, 6 is for Ox, 7 is for Skelm, 8 is for Pig, 9 is for Moon, 10 is for Egg, 11 is for Car, 12 is for Granny, 13 is for Big Fish, 14 is for Dead Woman, 15 is for Slegte Vrou, 16 is for Pigeon – Amajuba, 17 . . . Diamond Lady!

(*Enter* JAKES.)

JAKES: You are the Diamond Lady and I'm Jakes!

RUTH: Thank God! I was beginning to think I was at the wrong place.

MINGUS: How do you know you're at the right place?

JAKES: I'd like you to meet Mingus . . .

RUTH: How do you do?

JAKES: Mingus's lady friend, Princess . . .

RUTH: Hullo.

JAKES: This is Mr Fahfee . . .

RUTH: Hullo.

JAKES: Lulu over there . . .

RUTH: Hullo.

JAKES: This is the Mama of the house . . .

RUTH: Hullo.

JAKES: And Charlie I believe you've met.

(CHARLIE *has been pawing at* RUTH'*s shoes right through the introductions.*)

RUTH: Yes!

MINGUS: Com'on Charlie, back off! Listen Jakes – if you're making trouble again . . .

JAKES: There's going to be no trouble. This young lady has bravely stepped into the unknown. Jumped in where angels even fear to tread. Answered an unusual advert – and here she is. We are going to do everything we can to make life easy for her. I assure you, Ruth – you have the best protection in the neighbourhood. Mingus here is an American.

RUTH: An American!

MINGUS: An American. Nobody troubles an American's friends. But I choose my friends very very carefully!

MAMARITI: Lulu!

(LULU *crosses to her mother, who whispers in her ear, gesticulating furiously.*)

LULU: My mother wants to know if you can pay a good rent.

RUTH: A good rent? I'm sure I can.

(*Whispered exchange.*)

LULU: My mother wants to know if you can pay £2 5s a month?

RUTH: It's a bit steep.

LULU: So?

RUTH: Well, I can do it . . .

(*Whispered exchange.*)

LULU: My mother says you can stay.

RUTH: Thank you.

MINGUS: Hold it! Hold it! I'll decide. (*He takes a long walk around her, evaluating her.*) Alright, she can stay.

LULU: Yay!

JAKES: I knew it would work out. You'll stay with me of course. I've got a room at the back.

RUTH: I beg your pardon?

(PRINCESS *bursts out laughing, long and loud.*)

MINGUS: What you laughing at? I didn't bring you here to laugh at our guests.

PRINCESS: Ha! This Jewish is going to stay in the back with the situation. This I want to see.

MINGUS: Luister – watch out . . . watch out!

RUTH: 'Scuse me – I really don't think it's such a good idea to share a room – I hardly know you.

JAKES: It's quite alright. There's a curtain I'll put up.

RUTH: On the telephone you said I could have a room all to myself.

PRINCESS: A room all to yourself! Are you some kind of a moegoe?

RUTH: I beg your pardon!

PRINCESS: No one lives in a room to themselves here. You think this is Yeoville?

RUTH: But I can't just move in with a man I've hardly met. Look, I can pay a reasonable rent.

MAMARITI: Ja . . . Lulu.

(LULU *crosses over to her.*)

LULU: (*After whispered exchanges.*) My mother wants to know if you can bring spirits from town.

RUTH: Spirits from town?

LULU: Ja, spirits . . . whiskey, brandy, gin . . .

RUTH: Oh yes, I can do that.

Scene 2 15

JAKES: Hey, Fahfee!

LULU: My mother wants to know if you can help me with my homework.

RUTH: Yes!

LULU: Yay! My mother says you can sleep in her room.

RUTH: Thank you.

MINGUS: Ja, you can sleep in Lulu's bed.

LULU: Hey!

RUTH: Where will Lulu sleep?

MAMARITI: With me!

LULU: Ag Ma!

JAKES: There we are. No problems – I told you. It's simple. Spirits for the front room. Rent for the bedroom. Homework for the kitchen and stories for the backroom.

PRINCESS: And Mingus, perfume for the Princess!

MINGUS: Ag my sweetie, anything for you.

RUTH: I'll bring you perfume from John Orr's, if you want.

MINGUS: There you are, everything's gonna be just fine. Dis khuvet onder die korset.

RUTH: See, I'm the easiest person in the world to please. I'm happy with the simplest things. All I need is a light to read by, somewhere to sleep and a place to bath.

(*Everyone exclaims incredulously.*)

MINGUS: Charlie! Go out there and find me a bath!

(*Lights change. The cast set up a rhythm of typewriters with body and sound as the following song is chanted by* JAKES.)

> I said to Dam-Dam, Hoozit ou Dam-Dam?
> I said to Dam-Dam, What's been going on?
>
> He said to me, Oh, Jackie Boy, Jackie Boy,
> He said to me, I'm looking for my dream girl.

I said to Dam-Dam, Come on ou Dam-Dam,
Whatever happened to the dazzling Boksburg blonde?

He said to me, Oh Jackie Boy, Jackie Boy,
He said to me, I'm a sucker, I've been conned.

My love's not for sale – she's been messing me around,
Showbiz is my biz, not no lover's hunting-ground.

I said to Dam-Dam, Come on ou Dam-Dam,
Whatever happened to the nut-brown from Softown?

He said to me, Oh Jackie Boy, Jackie Boy,
You know a juicy berry when she's hanging on your neck.

I said to Dam-Dam, Come on ou Dam-Dam,
Dam-Dam is the biggest playboy in the plek.

He said to me, Oh Jackie Boy, Jackie Boy,
If she's not in town, she's just coaldust off my feet.

I said to Dam-Dam, Come on ou Dam-Dam,
Have you seen the Jewish girl who's living down the street?

(*Blackout.*)

Act 1   Scene 3

(LULU *is sitting on the floor trying to learn 'The Daffodils' by Wordsworth.* JAKES *watches as* MINGUS *and* PRINCESS *quarrel.* MAMARITI *sits quietly in a corner.* FAHFEE *sits at the kitchen table working on his gambling numbers.*)

PRINCESS: Ek soek haar nie hier nie. Mingus, hoe kan jy so maak? Let this Jewish girl just move in? As jou my like, Mingus, you'll get rid of her.

MINGUS: Listen my angel, my princess, ek mnca jou, okay, but you're driving me mad. If you don't shaddup I'll have to crack you up.

PRINCESS: How can you let her stay here? We don't know who she is. You don't listen to me – you only listen to Jakes.

MINGUS: Look – you're just an American's tjerrie, and that means you shaddup and listen or I'll have to cut you up.

PRINCESS: I know about these Jewish girls from Yeoville. They're spoilt. Their fathers give them lots of money – they do what they like. They've all got nannies. Well, I'm not going to be anybody's nanny.

LULU: You're just jealous.

MINGUS: Look, I brought you here. I give you dresses, I take you to bioscope, you're my princess. What else do you want?

PRINCESS: I want that Jewish girl out.

MINGUS: Shaddup or I'll have to cut your spinal off! I didn't bring you from your shack so you can complain.

LULU: I like her. I stared at her face all night. It glowed in the dark. It made me think of the line in this poem, 'a host of golden daffodils'. I need help with this homework.

PRINCESS: I'll help you.

LULU: What do you know – you're just an American's tjerrie.

PRINCESS: I'll give you a good klap. How can you let her stay here? She doesn't belong here, man. She's a European. Europeans don't live in Sophiatown. It's a native location.

JAKES: It's a freehold suburb – no fences, no superintendent.

MINGUS: Ja, and this house is open. If I say she stays, she stays.

JAKES: Look, she's got guts. I need her. She's a hot story. How many others are there like her?

LULU: There's that white woman living with the police sergeant in Orlando.

JAKES: Regina Brooks.

MINGUS: Ja, she's alright.

LULU: And there's the Afrikaans girl living with the Olifants in Ray Street.

MINGUS: I think she's a relative.

FAHFEE: A relative?

MINGUS: Ja, a relative.

JAKES: And here's Ruth Golden.

PRINCESS: Ja, and what are you going to say when the G-men raid? 'Make way for the Jewish – she's a new kind of girl.' Just pretend you don't see her?

JAKES: We'll hide her like we hide the booze.

PRINCESS: And who's gonna protect her from the Americans at night?

MINGUS: Me.

PRINCESS: But you are an American, wena.

MINGUS: I'll protect her.

PRINCESS: And the Berliners, and the Gestapo Gang, and the Vultures? Where have you ever seen a white girl in this Sophiatown – where?

FAHFEE: There are always Europeans here – drinking at the Back of the Moon, drinking at the Thirty-Nine Steps. In the nightclubs, in the jazz clubs, at the House of Truth, in the bioscope. What difference if one of them spends the night. Nobody's gonna know. And if they did, nobody'd give a damn.

MINGUS: Except for the Boere.

LULU: And the Princess!

PRINCESS: (*Chasing* LULU *around the room.*) You just watch your mouth!

LULU: Princess of the slum! Princess of the slum!

PRINCESS: Mingus!

MINGUS: Lulu! Tsama hansi! Sit down!

PRINCESS: How can you let her stay here? What does she want here? Is she an angel?

JAKES: I think this young lady's gonna do just fine. She'll help Lulu – and we'll be the talk of the town.

LULU: (*Flopping down.*) Ag – I'm finished with school. I hate it. What do they teach us? Nothing! How to be good Christian girls. Rubbish!

MINGUS: You're staying right there. Nobody says Mingus lets his sister on the streets. This house wants a situation – a B.A. Intellectual!

LULU: You've got your situation.

MINGUS: Where?

LULU: This Jewish girl's your situation. I'm going to be a film star – like Dolly Rathebe in 'African Jim' and 'The Magic Garden'.

(*She gets up and sings an extract from one of Dolly Rathebe's films.*)
'I came to Joburg, to the Golden City,
What did I come here for?'

(*The household applauds. Enter* RUTH.)

RUTH: Morning.

JAKES: Hullo Ruth. How did you sleep?

RUTH: Fine.

MINGUS: Are you sure?

RUTH: Yes.

JAKES: Was the bed alright?

RUTH: Yes, fine.

LULU: You were talking in your sleep.

RUTH: Was I?

LULU: Yes. I was watching your face. Did you have nightmares?

RUTH: I don't know.

LULU: I think you were talking about Yeoville.

RUTH: Was I?

LULU: Yes.

RUTH: It must have been the dogs.

MINGUS: The dogs?

RUTH: Yes.

MINGUS: What do you mean, the dogs?

RUTH: Well, the barking kept me awake.

LULU: And Mama's snoring!

MAMARITI: Eh wena! Hai! Wena ungakhulumi umswanila nxa!

MINGUS: Charlie! Get rid of those dogs!

RUTH: No, no. Please it's alright . . .

MINGUS: I'll stone them. I'll shoot them.

RUTH: No, please, it's quite alright really. It'll just take a bit of getting used to. There are dogs in Yeoville too.

JAKES: Of course, yes.

RUTH: You see, I'm just not used to sleeping three in a room.

MINGUS: Jakes, I want you out your room.

JAKES: What?

MINGUS: For the Jewish girl.

RUTH: No, please. Really it's alright.

MINGUS: (*Turning on her.*) Don't you argue with me.

JAKES: Listen Mingus, give it a few days. I'm sure everything will settle down.

MINGUS: Look here, Jakes, she's a European and a guest and in my house she gets the best.

RUTH: Please, I just want to be like everybody else.

PRINCESS: Well, you never will be!

RUTH: Now that is very unfair! You told me I'd have a room on my own and I'd hardly be in the house at all, and now already there's a whole fuss.

MINGUS: Listen, if you go back to Yeoville and tell everybody you were uncomfortable here, I'll be very much and extremely upset. I want you in Jakes' room.

RUTH: And where will Jakes sleep?

MINGUS: In the front room – on the floor – under his table, I don't know. Charlie! Where the hell is he?

PRINCESS: What are you doing here anyway?

RUTH: Curiosity?

PRINCESS: What?

(*Enter* CHARLIE, *flustered*.)

CHARLIE: Outside!

MINGUS: Where the hell have you been?

CHARLIE: Outside.

MINGUS: I want you out there tonight with the Baby B and stones. I want those goddamn dogs dead.

CHARLIE: Outside!

MINGUS: What?

CHARLIE: Outside.

(CHARLIE *and* MINGUS *exit. Re-enter* MINGUS.)

MINGUS: Fahfee, Jakes – outside!

(*The men exit.*)

PRINCESS: Already you're causing disruptions.

22 Act 1

MAMARITI: Hey Princess – leave the Jewish girl alone. I want her here and that's that. Don't you come here with your Princess nonsense.

(*The men enter carrying a large bath.*)

MINGUS: Jislaaik – it's heavy!

LULU: A bath! What we going to do with it? Tie it to the water tap outside?

MINGUS: You are going to fill it with hot water from the stove.

PRINCESS: Where are we going to put this stupid thing?

MINGUS: In the kitchen! And you shaddup.

RUTH: For heaven's sake! I didn't realize. The last thing I wanted was a special bath. I've had enough baths at home.

JAKES: We'll all use it.

MINGUS: Ja.

PRINCESS: I'm not going near that thing.

LULU: Me neither.

MINGUS: Ma?

MAMARITI: No.

MINGUS: Ma, shall we try it for size?

MAMARITI: Never! Not me, never!

MINGUS: Lulu.

LULU: No!

MINGUS: Lulu!

(MINGUS *signals to* CHARLIE, *who dumps* LULU *in the bath.* FAHFEE *attempts to intervene but his back is damaged from the weight of the bath.*)

RUTH: Charlie, I'm very sorry – I really didn't mean you to go to all that trouble.

MINGUS: Hey! Never, never apologize to Charlie. Understand? He does everything I say. Just keep your damn nose clean.

PRINCESS: Ja Mingus, tell her.

JAKES: Ruth Golden – now the bath's here, somebody's got to use it. And by all accounts it had better be you!

RUTH: I couldn't . . . I really couldn't.

(*The Cast sing 'Tobiansky'.*)

> Tobiansky (4)
> Why did you do this thing to me?
>
> You gave me freehold suburbs
> You gave me title deeds
> You gave me eveything
> A Softown majieta needs
> And then you take it away
>
> Tobiansky (3)
> Why did you do this thing to me?
>
> You gave me Odin bioscope
> You gave me Gerty Street
> You gave me Softown lifestyle
> And everything is sweet
> And then you take it away

(*There is a moment of transition as the bath is moved to one side of the stage.*)

FAHFEE: This bath is so big, I think the whole of Gerty Street will have to come and bath in here.

JAKES: Fahfee, watter nommer sal die Chinaman trek vanaand?

FAHFEE: (*Indicating the bath.*) 22 – American Battleship.

JAKES: (*Turning to the audience.*) Well, things settled down and within weeks Ruth seemed like part of the family. She wouldn't use the bath and so Mamariti started brewing great quantities of beer in it. I was planning my big break with Drum – dreaming of a double page full of pictures.

All those guys thought Ruth was great but I suspected they were just after any white girls. White skin, it's a fatal attraction. Heartbreak and humiliation. I was keeping my distance, as always, just watching.

Ruth wanted to move around with more freedom, so we let her in on some secrets.

(*Lights change.*)

Act 1   Scene 4

(RUTH *is having lessons in how to survive in Sophiatown from* JAKES, FAHFEE *and* MINGUS.)

FAHFEE: Ek sê, waar's die ouens hier?

RUTH: Hoozit gents!

FAHFEE: Is khuvet onder die korset – en met jou?

RUTH: Die mission is grand.

FAHFEE: En wie is jy?

RUTH: Ek! Ek is die matara van die dla!

FAHFEE: Wie?

RUTH: Die matara van die dla.

FAHFEE: Jy's mooi hey.

RUTH: Don't touch. Jy moenie baaiza nie. Sit gents. Sit julle majietas. Die magrizin van die stuk is nie hier nie.

FAHFEE: Wie?

RUTH: Die magrizin van die stuk?

MINGUS: Not bad, Fahfee, try it again.

FAHFEE: Ek sê, waar's die ouens hier?

RUTH: Hoozit gents!

FAHFEE: Is khuvet onder die korset – en met jou?

RUTH: Die mission is grand.

Scene 4 25

FAHFEE: En wie is jy?

RUTH: Ek! Ek is die matara van die dla!

FAHFEE: Wie?

RUTH: Die matara van die dla.

FAHFEE: Jy's mooi hey.

RUTH: Don't touch. Jy moenie baaiza nie. Sit gents. Sit julle majietas. Die magrizin van die stuk is nie hier nie.

FAHFEE: Wie?

RUTH: Die magrizin van die stuk?

MINGUS: Right. Grand. And if die majietas kom, and go for you, what do you say?

RUTH: I'm a virtuous well-bred girl, I'm a nylon.

MINGUS: And if they don't leave you alone, they really go for you . . .?

RUTH: Julle moenie baaiza nie?

MINGUS: Ag! Nee man!

RUTH: I don't know – I'll never learn.

JAKES: Look, it's in the eyes, it's a warning signal which says, 'Leave me alone.' It's because you're white. White flesh, it's a fatal attraction. They get you into bed – it's a fart in the face for this Prime Minister Strijdom.

MINGUS: Look, if an American comes in here and he wants you, what are you going to do?

RUTH: I'll stop him.

MINGUS: These Americans always get what they want. They see girls and they're mad, mad. They see white girls and they're over the back of the moon. And white girls living in Softown! It's our territory, man. I see something, I go for it. Look at me and Princess. I klapped her till she loved me.

RUTH: Mingus!

MINGUS: The more you love, the more you hit. Now she'll never leave me alone. So, if an American comes in here and goes for you what are you going to do?

RUTH: I don't know. I'll just go back to Yeoville.

FAHFEE: Go back to Yeoville?

RUTH: You want me to learn a whole new language, and you want me to have a special look in my eye, and you want to klap me until I love you. I think I must be mad to even try.

FAHFEE: You're giving up!

RUTH: Look, I come from an ordinary Jewish family. We've lived in Yeoville for as long as I can remember.

FAHFEE: And now you're going back!

RUTH: I'm trying to change my whole life!

FAHFEE: But you're giving up!

RUTH: I'm tired!

MINGUS: You're tired! What's the matter? Jakes' room not good enough for you? Charlie! Charlie! I told you to get rid of those goddamn dogs!

RUTH: Look – I don't want you to call Charlie. That's one of the reasons I'm tired. Every time a little thing goes wrong – Charlie! Charlie! I'll sort things out for myself.

MINGUS: You're bloody ungrateful. Why don't you bath? I brought it specially for you.

RUTH: You did not! Charlie did!

MINGUS: I told him to go out and get it.

JAKES: Look gents, we want life easy for the lady but not so easy she leaves. If she doesn't want to bath, she doesn't have to. If the dogs keep her awake at night that's tough. If the Americans want her – well, that's how it is. Come on, Miss Golden, cheer up . . . come on . . . smile. The sky can fall on your head anywhere. Come on, we'll take you to Freedom

Square, we'll show you the Back of the Moon, we'll take you to Can Themba's House of Truth and we'll teach you hoe om te wietie . . . Does that make you feel better? Hey, Fahfee, why don't we try that little bit of lingo again?

FAHFEE: (*Clowning for her.*) Torch, torch daai wiebit. Torch daai tjerrie. Ek hak jou. Kom my little matara. Ons wietie, ek en jy. Kom, ons moet Katz en Lourie. As ek jou magrizin request, sal jy my trou?

JAKES: Say, 'Yes.'

RUTH: Yes.

(FAHFEE *laughs,* RUTH *gives him a punch.*)

FAHFEE: Kom, ons moet Katz en Lourie. Life is 'n boogie. Dis singalie. Dis khuvet onder the korset. I'll show you Kofifi, I'll show you Maklera. Ons sal in die main road pedestrie and al die moemishes sal stare, en jy sal die matara van die dla wees. Jy notch?

RUTH: Sure I notch. (*To* JAKES.) What's he saying?

MINGUS: In a nutshell he'd like to Katz en Lourie you.

JAKES: Which constitutes a rather unexpectedly early offer of marriage – considering that he's just met you.

RUTH: (*Playing along.*) Hey, hey don't touch. Jy moenie baaiza nie. I'll give you such a zetz. Sit julle gents, sit julle majietas en die larnie van die stuk will get you a brandy.

FAHFEE: Mahok.

RUTH: A larnie's a white girl, right?

FAHFEE: Ja, a smart white person like you.

JAKES: But you're Jewish, right?

RUTH: So Nu? What's Jewish? I don't know what the hell I am. I'm Jewish on Mondays, I'm White on Tuesdays, I'm South African on Wednesdays, I'm a Democrat on Thursdays, and I'm confused on all the other days. Mostly I'm just confused.

JAKES: What the hell am I? The Boere want us in separate locations, but what am I? I speak Zulu, Xhosa, Sotho, English, Afrikaans, and in moments of weakness I even speak Tsotsitaal.

FAHFEE: Hey! Tsotsitaal! Dis die taal van die ouens. It's a sophisticated taal.

JAKES: So who the hell am I?

FAHFEE: Vra jou ma, man!

JAKES: I'm a would-be intellectual, living in a wasteland, with no power to change anything except words – and a fat lot of good they do!

MINGUS: (*Suddenly aggressive, jumps up and moves in on* RUTH.) Come on, we must teach you lang-arm dancing for the Ritz. Arm uit! Daai kant! Ga my skouer. (RUTH *does not understand.*) Ga my skouer, man! (RUTH *hesitates, then takes his shoulder. They take up a position for a waltz.*) And – one, two, three, one, two, three . . .

RUTH: (*Laughing.*) I can do this! This is just a European waltz.

MINGUS: (*Offended.*) Nee man. This is for the Ritz, Sophiatown style. And one, two, three. One, two, three. One, two, three. And the lights go low, and the jazz band plays slow, and you are my wiebit . . . my matara . . . Bite my neck . . . Bite my neck!

RUTH: Mingus!

MINGUS: Bite my neck!

RUTH: (*Pulling away.*) Please!

MINGUS: What's the matter? Don't you like to dance? Or maybe you don't like to dance with Mingus? Kom, fok met my, kom!

(MINGUS *chases* RUTH *around the room.*)

JAKES: Mingus! Mingus!

MINGUS: Shaddup, Jakes, man. She's got to learn, man. This

is not Yeoville here, man. It's rough here. You can't be a larnie and live here. You think your sweet polite words will save you? You think your sweet white words will protect you?

JAKES: Mingus!

MINGUS: Shaddup, Jakes! Here it's bicycle spokes, and jungles, and Baby Brownies, and Lugers. (*To* RUTH.) All nice European guns, mind you, from your war. It wasn't our war – it was your war. Look, look at my scars, look at my knife wounds – they're from our own war. You think Sophiatown is just jazz and clubs and the bright lights! It's a war, man – and you want to make this your war! Well, you've got lots to learn. And you can't pretend it's not happening because it will never go away. If you want to live here, white girl, you must learn – or pack up! Voetsak! Go back to Yeoville!

(*Blackout.*)

Act 1 Scene 5

(*A single tight spot reveals* RUTH *sitting in a chair.* FAHFEE *stands behind her. She listens with intense concentration, desperately trying to learn.*)

FAHFEE: (*in a monotone*) 1 is for King; 2, Monkey; 3, Seawater; 4, Dead Man; 5 is for Tiger; 6 is for Ox; 7 is for Skelm; 8 is for Pig; 9 is for Moon; 10, Eggs; 11, Car; 12, Granny; 13, Big Fish; 14, Dead Woman; 15, Slegte Vrou; 16, Pigeons; 17, Diamond Lady; 18, Small Change; 19, Small Girl; 20, Cat; 21, Elephant; 22, Ship; 23, Long Hair; 24, Big Mouth; 25, Big House; 26, Bees.

(*Blackout.*)

Act 1 Scene 6

(LULU *is working at her homework.* MAMARITI *is carefully cleaning the typewriter.* RUTH *is writing in a diary.*)

LULU: Homework, bloody homework! Every day is homework. Got to wash the dishes for Mama, look after the customers, but these school teachers, they don't understand.

RUTH: What are you doing?

LULU: I'm writing a composition.

RUTH: I'll help you.

LULU: Will you? You're a star, hey!

RUTH: What's it about?

LULU: It's called 'My Family'. God, my teachers are dumb – what a stupid title: 'My Family'!

RUTH: Well, what have you got there?

LULU: First I started writing about my mother.

RUTH: Mmmm?

LULU: She's just a cheeky old woman, breaking the law, working on her beer, and planning for her future which never comes.

MAMARITI: Sis! You stupid little idiot. How can you say all those things about me after all I've done for you?

LULU: Ag Ma, it's just a composition.

RUTH: And?

LULU: I'm also writing about my brother Mingus, who's always stealing goods from the railways.

RUTH: I'm not sure you should say those things.

LULU: But they're true!

RUTH: So?

LULU: Do you know, Mingus and the American gang, they stop the intellectuals, die situations, on the street corner, and to make trouble they make them recite Shakespeare!

RUTH: Shakespeare?

LULU: That's what Jakes told me. He says he's got a special line he learnt just in case,'Oh what a rogue and peasant slave am I'.

RUTH: Hamlet!

LULU: Ja. I was going to write it here but Jakes says I shouldn't – he says all my teachers will think it's bad English! So I just write, 'Mingus steals goods from the railways.'

RUTH: Surely there are nice things you can write?

LULU: My teacher says telling the truth is a virtue.

RUTH: But there are all sorts of truths. It's true to say your brother steals from the railways, but it's also true to say that he gives your mother money to run the house, and money for your school.

LULU: He can keep his money for school.

RUTH: No! He pays for you, why not tell that truth?

LULU: A thief is a thief is a thief!

MAMARITI: Hey shaddup! It's enough now. Mingus brings me money and he's my son. If you tell everybody he's a thief, whatever you've got that's nice, they'll just say it's stolen! Fool!

LULU: Okay Ma!

RUTH: Carry on.

LULU: I wrote here about Princess, who's so lazy.

RUTH: Lulu! There must be something else.

LULU: Well . . . I wrote about her being in jealousy about you.

RUTH: Lulu! There must be something you like about her – she's very pretty.

LULU: She thinks she's pretty – she's always working on her toenails. I think her toenails are bloody ugly!

RUTH: She gives you presents.

LULU: She gave me a present only once – when she first arrived. Now she thinks she's the madam of the house. And now I'm writing about Ruth Golden, who is this strange European lady nobody understands. She's always the centre of the attractions. She thinks if she comes to live here everything will be alright.

RUTH: And I'm writing about Lulu who is the cheekiest sixteen-year-old I know.

LULU: You know, when I first met you, I thought you were Regina Brooks.

RUTH: Ag, I look nothing like her. She's big and fat, and wears a doek!

LULU: How do you know what she looks like?

RUTH: I saw her in Jakes' magazine.

LULU: Everywhere in this house it's just fiction, fiction, fiction. Jakes told me he's writing all about you. He must be in love with you.

RUTH: Nonsense, Lulu!

LULU: Yes . . . He told me, he stares at your face and makes up the most fantastic stories. He tells me he's writing all about you, where you come from, what you're doing here . . .

RUTH: He knows none of those things!

LULU: That's what I told him. He told me he makes them up. I told him he's not allowed to, he told me he could. So, what are you doing here anyway?

RUTH: Let's just say I've got my own stories to write.

LULU: Fiction! I want the truth!

RUTH: Alright . . . I guess I just wanted to see what the other side of the world looked like.

LULU: And what do your parents think?

RUTH: My parents think I'm in Cape Town!

MAMARITI: Hayikhona!

RUTH: Ja Mama, they think I'm in Cape Town sorting out my life, and here I am in Sophiatown making it more confused.

LULU: You'll get caught in the end.

RUTH: I expect to.

LULU: So why don't you tell the truth?

RUTH: There are different sorts of truths, Lulu. Remember that.

(*Enter* MINGUS *and* PRINCESS. MINGUS *is wearing a trench coat, and chewing an apple. He also carries a Benzedrine sniffer which he sniffs constantly. His hat is low over his eyes. He is acting out the role of Styles in a scene from the film 'Street With No Name'.*)

(PRINCESS *follows as his henchman. She has a low-brimmed hat down over her eyes and an imaginary cigar clutched in her fingers. They both speak in ridiculously exaggerated American accents.*)

PRINCESS: (*Offstage.*) Alright, Styles, so just tell me what we gotta do.

LULU: Mingus and Princess have been to the movies! (*She and* RUTH *hide.*)

MINGUS: There's only one guy who's the brain of this outfit, and that's me!

PRINCESS: Right, boss. Just tell me what we gotta do.

MINGUS: First Ginger Girl, just give your daddy a big kiss and then get out a map.

(*She leans over and gives him an elegant kiss, then spreads an imaginary map on the table.* MINGUS *studies it.*)

Alright! If we're gonna hit this place, we've gotta hit it hard. So when I give the word (*Sniffs.*), you go that end and I go this end. Scarface covers the rear. (*Sniffs.*) Now remember, when the hit comes out, no shooting till I say. (*Sniffs.*) I'm de brains of this outfit, and that brooks no contradiction. (*He takes a hefty bite from the apple.*)

PRINCESS: That was a sweet job you pulled in Pittsburgh.

MINGUS: No conviction . . .

PRINCESS: And that was a nice little shooting match in Miami.

MINGUS: No conviction . . .

PRINCESS: And that was a very surprising incident in Chicago.

MINGUS: No conviction . . .

(*Enter* JAKES.)

JAKES: Hey, Modimo wa khotso. What's going on?

(LULU *bursts out of hiding.*)

LULU: Mingus and Princess have been to the bioscope! Mingus and Princess have been to Balansky's.

PRINCESS: The Odin, wena.

LULU: Mingus and Princess think they're in the movies. Miami – no conviction! (*Mocking* MINGUS, *she snorts.*) Chicago – no conviction. (*Snorts.*) Softown – no conviction! (*Snorts.*)

MINGUS: I'll give you a blerry klap, man. Shaddup!

JAKES: So what did you see?

MINGUS: 'Street With No Name.' Starring Richard Widmark as Styles. God, I'm a new man. From now on, I plan all my robberies with a map. Nothing but the best for Mingus. Nothing can stop me. I rob from the rich and sell to the poor. There's no limit, man . . . White girl, if you live here, you don't say a word.

RUTH: Cross my heart I never will.

(*Enter* FAHFEE.)

FAHFEE: (*Agitated.*) What's the number! What's the number! Number 4 – Dead Man, trouble. Number 26 – Bees, trouble. It's number 27 – Dogs, policemen, trouble.

JAKES: What's the matter, Fahfee?

FAHFEE: I dream of number 8 – the Pig, the white man, and I bring news.

JAKES: What news? Is there a story?

FAHFEE: There's a story, but will Drum tell this story? It's the end for us.

JAKES: Come, Fahfee, tell your story.

FAHFEE: They're moving us out! Hulle sê die Native Resettlement Act of 1954 sê die hele families wat hier in Kofifi pola, hulle moet klerrie. Hulle sê daar's accommodation in die new location van Meadowlands.

JAKES: Did you get it?

FAHFEE: Yes. Toby Street. They say the first moves are on 12th February.

JAKES: Are you sure about this, Fahfee?

FAHFEE: See for yourself. Notices.

JAKES: How many families?

FAHFEE: One five two.

RUTH: Jakes, what are you going to do?

JAKES: I don't know. Write the story. What else can I do?

FAHFEE: Congress says we mustn't move. We must resist, like in the Defiance Campaign. Congress calls for five thousand volunteers. We've got a plan.

JAKES: The secret M-Plan?

FAHFEE: Ja.

RUTH: How does it work?

JAKES: Nobody knows – it's a secret.

FAHFEE: (*Suddenly suspicious.*) Why do you want to know?

RUTH: Pardon?

MINGUS: Ja, why do you want to know?

FAHFEE: Why do you want to know?

RUTH: That's great! That's really great. You don't trust me.

FAHFEE: You must earn your trust – you must work.

RUTH: What must I do?

FAHFEE: Stop all this shit.

RUTH: How do you expect me to do that?

FAHFEE: My uncle has been here since 1924. He knows nothing else – and now they want to move him to this Meadowlands. Ons dak nie. Ons pola hier!

JAKES: And what do you do when the policemen come?

FAHFEE: Die G-men?

JAKES: Ja.

FAHFEE: We've got a plan.

JAKES: But you hardly know what it is!

FAHFEE: When the time is right, we'll hear.

JAKES: It sounds very unsatisfactory to me.

FAHFEE: I don't care! I'd rather die than move from this place. They can kill us one by one, but we won't move. We'll sit down in the streets and wait for the bullets. There's going to be a war. Petitions, letters, committees – it's rubbish! I'm telling you, it's rubbish. There must be blood. Then things will happen.

MINGUS: (*To* RUTH *in a moment of great anger.*) And it will be your blood!

RUTH: Jakes, please – I can't stand this.

MINGUS: Ja, just run back to Yeoville.

FAHFEE: What am I going to do in this Meadowlands? How am I going to put bread in my mouth? What's going to happen to my business with the Chinaman, the Gong? Where's he gonna be when they move Sophia? And the Indians? And the caureds? Where's the jazz? Where's the life? Where's the situations? Where's the teachers? Where's the life? Where's the Fahfee? Where's the life? It's just dust and blood and dust!

MINGUS: Go back to Yeoville!

(*Change of lights. The Cast sing 'Meadowlands' in a slow and melancholy waltz time. Then the rhythm changes to an up-tempo jive and they launch into a lively dance.*)

MEADOWLANDS

Otla utlwa makgowa a re
A re yeng ko Meadowlands (2)
Meadowlands Meadowlands
Meadowlands sithandwa sam' (2)

Otla utlwa botsotsi ba re
Ons dak nie ons pola hier (2)
Pola hier pola hier
Pola hier sithandwa sam' (2)

(You'll hear the whites say
Let's move to Meadowlands (2)
Meadowlands Meadowlands
Meadowlands, my love (2)

You'll hear the tsotsis say
We're not moving, we're staying here (2)
Stay here, stay here
Stay here, my love) (2)

Act 1   Scene 7

(*The family are gathered around the kitchen table.* JAKES *flourishes a* Drum *magazine with great pride and excitement.*)

JAKES: I've got it! (*He lays the magazine on the table.*) I've got it here! Come and see, come right up and see! This is break. No more boxing, no more gangster stories. I'm dealing with socialites. Come on – open it. Who do you see?

LULU: (*Opening it.*) It's Ruth!

RUTH: (*Rushing to look.*) Do I really look like that?

LULU: Look here, it's me! Oh, Jakes, in my school uniform! How could you do that to me?

PRINCESS: (*Pleased with herself.*) Look what I look like!

JAKES: The front page of Drum is waiting! Cheesecake, crime, babies, boxing – and more cheesecake. Princess must become a Drum girl, a model.

PRINCESS: Do you really think so?

MINGUS: You'll be famous, my sweetie. Let's have a party.

EVERYONE: Ja!

JAKES: Don't you want to hear it? Listen here: 'The first of four articles on a Sophiatown phenomenon, "Ruth Golden" by Jakes Mamabolo.'

RUTH: God – if my parents find out they'd die!

LULU: Come on. Who in Yeoville reads Drum? It's a native magazine.

FAHFEE: Don't worry – nobody is gonna find out. Jakes, what's the page number?

JAKES: What?

FAHFEE: The page number, what's it man? It's today's winner.

JAKES: Number 23!

FAHFEE: Ah! You see! Number 23! A Dream of Long Hair!

JAKES: Don't you want to hear what it says?

FAHFEE: Com'on, give it here – I'll read it. '*Mixing It Up in Softown*. Dig that crazy white girl living it up in Gerty Street! Pshoo! Was there a scramble when word went round

Sophiatown that a Jewish girl was living at Mamariti's Diamond Shebeen . . .'

MAMARITI: Say that again – that's me!

FAHFEE: 'Nobody believed it was possible. Was this just a fantasy? A Jewish girl living in Softown! It's not possible. Is she crazy as a bedbug? Who'd leave the easy white life of Yeoville for the seething hot-spots of Kofifi? Well, folks, let me introduce you. She is none other than Ruth Golden. Height: five foot three inches . . .'

RUTH: Five foot four!

JAKES: Oops! Sorry.

FAHFEE: Aah . . . Five foot four. 'Long black hair pulled back in a swinging switch. A pert but comfortable figure. Curious bright eyes . . .'

RUTH: Come on!

FAHFEE: 'She tells me . . .'

JAKES: Uh, uh – that's my bit. 'She tells me she worked at Vanguard's, the bookshop, and we all know what happens there! Could she be an eager intellectual? A wide-eyed jazz maniac? A demure but daring do-gooder? Or is it just an advertising stunt?'

RUTH: Jakes!

JAKES: 'Hey no man, Ruth Golden's just a gal with a golden heart. With her sweet smile and her helpful ways, she's become a smash-hit attraction at Mamariti's Diamond Shebeen.'

MAMARITI: God, me again? I'm famous!

JAKES: 'Says Ma: "She's the best whiskey-glass washer I've had in ten years."'

MAMARITI: I never said that!

LULU: Ag, Ma. It doesn't have to be true!

JAKES: Listen! 'Says Princess, "She's not so bad."'

PRINCESS: (*Magnanimously.*) You're not so bad.

JAKES: 'But then I must add, Princess is not so bad herself. She's the other hot girl in the house. A girl with real style and you know these girls don't throw around the compliments. Mingus, that regular church-goer . . .'

MINGUS: What?

JAKES: Okay! Just kidding.

MINGUS: What you got written there?

JAKES: Just listen. 'Mingus, reputed to be one of the hot American Gang, says of our Jewish girl, "For someone of her complexion, she's got spunk. She's alright. She's hot!" And that's a hot compliment from Mingus. So there we are, against all the odds. A Jewish girl living in Sophiatown. Read in the next issue, in her own words, *How Ruth Golden Manages.*'

RUTH: How can you write all that, Jakes? There's just gonna be trouble.

JAKES: Nonsense. We've written about Regina Brooks, we've written about the Americans, we've written about politics. It's what people want to hear. And what's wrong with a Jewish girl living in Softown?

RUTH: There's nothing wrong. But it's illegal.

MINGUS: Look. We're two streets from Westdene. If the G-men come, you're out the door and up the road into the white suburbs in a tick.

RUTH: And all these other articles? I haven't said a word.

JAKES: You will. You will.

MINGUS: Come on, fok the G-men, let's have a big party! Mama, where's this week's booze?

MAMARITI: With the Jewish lady, of course.

MINGUS: Come on, get the booze! We're having a party.

(*The household breaks into a celebratory song.*)

>A bo tle
>Re ba kakqathe
>Ga bo pala
>Re bo tsho lole (2)
>
>Serope sa nqwanyana
>Ke Moseretsi
>Se bakela bashimane
>Dikqatatso (2)
>
>(Let it come
>We'll drink it
>If it doesn't taste nice
>We'll throw it out (2)
>
>Girls' thighs
>Are a lot of work
>They keep on causing problems
>For the guys) (2)

(RUTH *fetches bottles of gin, brandy and whiskey, hidden in brown-paper packets.* LULU *hands out glasses. The song gets raucous.* RUTH *interrupts.*)

RUTH: I've got a surprise! Along with the usual gift from the Yeoville shops: a bottle of special home-made Jewish Friday-night wine.

FAHFEE: What?

RUTH: I thought we might all like to try it. It's specially made for Friday night, and today's Friday, so here we are. Who knows, the entire house may be miraculously converted.

FAHFEE: Three drops of this Jewish wine and we're all Softown Majietas.

JAKES: Com'on then, let's hit that bottle. (*He opens the wine and pours.*) Right everybody, take a glass. We'll drink a toast in Jewish wine to the Jewish girl. And here's hoping for an instant rise in circulation.

MAMARITI: Hold it! Hold it! The man at the chemist shop says that we must say a prayer before we drink wine!

RUTH: Right – it's customary in Yeoville.

FAHFEE: A prayer? Ah . . . Please God don't make me too drunk tonight. Amen.

JAKES: I'll do it – just teach me how.

RUTH: It's in Hebrew.

MINGUS: Hebrew! Let's hear it.

RUTH: You really want to hear it?

EVERYONE: Yes!

RUTH: Alright. Everyone stand. Put your hat on your head, Mr Fahfee.
 Baruch Atah Adonai, Elohaynu Melech Ha'Olam.
 Borai Pri Hagafen. Amen.

FAHFEE: It sounds like Tsotsitaal!

JAKES: What does it mean?

RUTH: Praised be the Lord our God, King of the Universe, who gave us the fruit of the vine.

FAHFEE: Jy sien hier in Kofifi, ons kan nie drink voor die madlozis drink, and so ons maak so.

(*He pours some wine on the ground.* CHARLIE *attempts to catch it in his glass.*)

Hey man, Charlie, jy's nog nie 'n madlozi nie. Hulle moet eerste drink, ons kan nie alleen drink. Ons moet hulle koek gee. Hulle drink en hulle's alright!

RUTH: You spill some on the ground?

FAHFEE: Ja, vir die ancestors.

RUTH: We do the same! On Passover we leave the door open, and the ghost of Elijah's supposed to come in and drink the wine. I suppose it's the same thing really.

FAHFEE: Ghost?

RUTH: Ghost, Mr Fahfee.

LULU: What is this Passover?

RUTH: Passover? It's when the Jews were living in Egypt under the tyranny of a wicked Pharaoh and God said he'd send his angel of death to kill all the first-born. But he told the Jews if they'd put a sign on the door they'd be passed over.

MAMARITI: Perhaps we can also put a sign on our door.

MINGUS: No, no, it won't work here. We're all wicked.

JAKES: I suspect this good Lord couldn't give a damn, and even if he does, his voice is very distant. We'll have to fight it out for ourselves.

FAHFEE: You say this prayer is 'Blessed be the Lord our God, who made the wine'.

RUTH: Blessed be the Lord our God, King of the Universe, who gave us the fruit of the vine.

LULU: How many gods have you got?

RUTH: The Lord is One.

LULU: The Lord is one what?

RUTH: No, no. The Lord is One – unified.

LULU: In our church we say God is Three in One.

RUTH: I admit it is confusing.

MAMARITI: And the ancestors – there are many, many.

FAHFEE: I've got it! You say 'Blessed be the Lord because he's King of the Universe'? Blessed is die Lord want hy's die Baas van die Hele Joint. Hy's alles, want hy gee ons die vrugte vir die koek. Hy's alright! Ja, daar's net een religion en daar's net een taal; en daai's Tsotsitaal, Kofifi style.

MAMARITI: Ruthiwe, what is a Jewish? The only Jewish I know is the man in the chemist shop and one day he said to me, 'Meshugenah-kop chazer'. What is this 'Meshugenah-kop chazer'?

RUTH: Mama, you don't want to know that.

MAMARITI: Certainly I do.

RUTH: It means, 'Madman pig'.

MAMARITI: Is that nice? When will these white people learn?

LULU: So what is a Jewish?

RUTH: Well, it's really hard to say. It's not a religion, because you can be an unbeliever and still be Jewish. And it's not a nationality, because you can be South African and be Jewish. It's not even a language, because the only Hebrew I know is this Baruch Atah. Perhaps it's like a tribe. A lost tribe. It's very confusing.

JAKES: God is One, and God is Three, and the ancestors are many, and I speak Zulu and Xhosa and Tswana and English and Afrikaans and Tsotsitaal, and if I'm lucky Ruth will teach me Hebrew, and the Boere and the U.P. and the Congress fight it out, and this Softown is filled with Coloured and Indian and Chinese and Zulus . . . but this Jewish remains a mystery. And Softown is a brand-new generation and we are blessed with a perfect confusion.

MINGUS: Ruth Golden. Come here! I've got a little surprise for you.

RUTH: For me?

MINGUS: Charlie! Go and fetch that little box!

(*Exit* CHARLIE.)

RUTH: A surprise for me?

MINGUS: Ja, guess.

RUTH: I can't.

MINGUS: Come on, guess.

RUTH: I don't know. Sweets?

MINGUS: Come on. Better than that.

RUTH: Buttons? I'm really no good at guessing.

MINGUS: Again.

RUTH: Please, Mingus.

(MINGUS *takes the box from* CHARLIE, *who has returned. He conceals it from* RUTH.)

MINGUS: Come on. Pocket size. Guess!

RUTH: No, please, Mingus.

MINGUS: Pearls!

RUTH: Pearls! For me?

JAKES: Mingus, what you playing at?

MINGUS: Just a present from Mingus, Jakes.

RUTH: Gosh, Mingus, they're beautiful. I'll have to borrow one of Princess's gowns.

PRINCESS: You can't have one of my dresses.

RUTH: Ah . . . what's wrong, Princess?

PRINCESS: Absolutely nothing!

RUTH: Come on, Princess. What's wrong?

PRINCESS: There's nothing wrong.

MINGUS: Come, Princess – what's the matter?

PRINCESS: You ask me what's the matter? How can you give her pearls? (*To* RUTH.) I'm his girl.

RUTH: Come on, Princess. He's always giving you presents. Dresses, perfumes, jerseys. Oh my God, Mingus – where did you get them? You stole them! God, I'm drunk!

MINGUS: I did not steal them.

RUTH: Of course you did.

MINGUS: Nonsense. Somebody gave them to me.

RUTH: Ah . . . come on!

MINGUS: I'm telling you. I walk into the Ritz – me and my boys. We open the doors – the swing doors. Wam! Wam! And everybody's dancing. I stand for a moment. Very quiet. Just like Styles. I survey the scene from under my hat. And then – Ladies and Gentlemen, Mataras and Majietas, Dames en Here – the music's still playing – 'Blue Moon' – but nobody's dancing. They're all looking at me. I say, 'Ladies this side, Gents that side.' They're all up against the walls. And I walk to the gents, 'Ouens, steek julle linke hande uit.' And all the left hands shoot out, zip! Al die rappe. And as I walk I thank each one of them as I go by.

(*He saunters, hat in hand, reliving the collection of the watches.*)

And I walk up to the ladies. 'Yes ladies, let's see what you got. Show your necks.' And they showed! There were the pearls, big ones and little ones. And I say, 'Make your gifts,' and they make their gifts. And I walk, just like in church collections.

RUTH: I can't take them, Mingus. They're stolen goods.

MINGUS: You've never complained before.

RUTH: You've never given me anything before.

MINGUS: But you know what's going on here.

RUTH: It's none of my business.

PRINCESS: She won't take them, Mingus. She's too clean, too holy, too white. But I'll take them. (*She takes them.*)

RUTH: (*Snatching them back.*) I've changed my mind. I'll have them.

JAKES: Before you know it you'll be with him on the jobs.

(LULU *languidly falls off her chair.*)

LULU: This red wine is making me sad. I want to be Jewish. I want to be a princess. I want to be the centre of the attractions. I want to be like Dolly Rathebe and sing in all the movies.

(LULU *launches into a maudlin and drunken version of 'Stormy Weather'. Suddenly there is a violent knocking on the door.*)

FAHFEE: Oh my God! Dis die G-men! Vice en liquor squad!

JAKES: Ruth! You must hide!

RUTH: God! Where?

FAHFEE: Get rid of the bottles!

LULU: You must run to Westdene!

PRINCESS: Hide in the cupboard, with the dresses.

JAKES: You must just get out!

RUTH: Jakes, please, you must come with me.

JAKES: I can't. Just move! (RUTH *moves out.*)

MINGUS: Fok julle G-men! Die is onse plek!

JAKES: Shut up, Mingus. Mama, open the door.

MAMARITI: Not me!

JAKES: Lulu!

LULU: No!

JAKES: Listen, Lulu, you're a schoolchild, you're an innocent.

LULU: I've had too much of this Jewish wine.

JAKES: Go to the door, play the innocent. Get them to fok off. Tell them you're doing homework.

(LULU *reluctantly exits.* CHARLIE *follows. There is more frantic cleaning up. Re-enter* LULU.)

LULU: Mama, it's a special notice for you.

MAMARITI: Read it.

LULU: 'You are hereby required in terms of the Native Resettlement Act of 1954 to vacate the premises in which you reside. The date given is February 12th. You will be offered accommodation in the new location of Meadowlands.'

(*Enter* CHARLIE.)

CHARLIE: I'm going to get a house!

(*Blackout.*)

Act 2   Scene 1

(*The company storms onto stage, singing 'Koloi e'. Each character emerges and shouts his or her protest over the music.*)

KOLOI E

Koloi e, ha ena marili (2)
Ha e tsamaya, ya nyahyatha
Ha e tsamaya, e etsa 'Chips' (2)

Sutha sutha wena Strijdom
Ha o sa suthe
Sutha sutha wena Strijdom
Ha o sa suthe
E ya go gata!

(This car, this car
Has no wheels (2)
When it moves, it moves quietly
When it moves,
It dances 'Chips' (2)

Give way, give way, you Strijdom
If you don't
It will ride over you!)

MINGUS: Strijdom, Strijdom, watch out! Watch out, Strijdom!

FAHFEE: Hey, hey, hey, hey, hey! Die kar van ons – it's going right over you!

CHARLIE: Ja Strijdom. Ons dak nie, ons pola hier. Gee pad, gee pad, gee pad!

PRINCESS: Hey Boere, watch out! This car it's got no wheels! Gee pad, gee pad!

JAKES: Strijdom, get your ox-wagon out the way! Strijdom – get, get, get!

FAHFEE: Our children, born here, in Gerty Street, in Ray Street, in Good Street, in Gold Street. Don't think you can drive us away Strijdom!

MINGUS: We're here to stay. Dis onse plek. Voetsak, voetsak, voetsak!

LULU: Title deeds. En nou waar's die law? Fok jou law, Strijdom. Dis 'n rich man's law.

JAKES: Get your Boere out. The rivers are running. Take your guns, take your Saracens en gaan weg. Give way Strijdom, give way.

MAMARITI: Here we come, Strijdom. Watch out, this car's moving! It's got no wheels. Here we come. We're gonna roll, we're gonna roll right over you.

MINGUS: Kom Boere, gee pad, gee pad, gee pad!

FAHFEE: Strijdom, remember the Defiance Campaign. Ons is in Defiance. Ten thousand people broke your rubbish laws. Boere gee pad, gee pad, gee pad. Ons pola hier! Gee pad.

(*The song builds as the Cast prepare for the next scene.* RUTH *and* MAMARITI *seat themselves at the kitchen table and cut vegetables.* LULU *resumes her studies and* JAKES *sits at his typewriter. The song ends.*)

FAHFEE: News of the Day! Dikgang tsa gompieno! Congress calls for a fight on all fronts. This year is the year of the Congress of the People. We won't move. What's the number? Yes? Yes? It's 26. 26 June 1955 – one nine five five.

JAKES: Hey Fahfee, what's going on?

FAHFEE: You must keep up, Mr Drum. The magic number is 26.

RUTH: Bees.

FAHFEE: That's right. What kind of South Africa do you want? Write it on a piece of paper, any paper – Drum Magazine, Star, New Age, school books. Everybody must have an answer. We are going to make a new South Africa. These Boere be damned!

MAMARITI: That's right.

FAHFEE: This is a big day for news. Congress calls for a total boycott of all schools.

LULU: Agreed! I'm not going back to school any more.

RUTH: No more school?

FAHFEE: That's right.

MAMARITI: Hau, Lulu.

LULU: I don't want this Bantu education, Mama. It's for the gutter.

FAHFEE: Verwoerd's new Bantu Education is for slaves. This is 1955. We want education for freedom. Father Huddleston says, 'Close the church schools rather than teach children rubbish.'

MAMARITI: Hey wena. I don't care what he says – I want my child back at school.

FAHFEE: Hey Mamawe. They're coming with this new education. They want to move us. Well, I'm telling you, this is just the beginning – the tip on top of the mountain. And what are we doing about it? What are you doing about it, yes, you Mama? And you, my broer? You just let them stomp all over you . . . Well, no-one's going to stomp on me, they can come with their lorries, their guns and their bulldozers, but they won't find me. Ba tla bona marago a noga!

LULU: Ja, they can try to force us back into the classrooms, but we won't move. They can keep their gutter education. These Boere are trying to take over the country.

MAMARITI: Hey Lulu, you don't talk like that.

FAHFEE: Lulu is right, Mama. I'm not going to be anybody's slave.

MAMARITI: Hey wena, Fahfee. What's gone wrong with you?

FAHFEE: I am recruited.

JAKES: Recruited? That sounds like a story.

FAHFEE: I am a freedom volunteer. I am one of thousands.

The working people of this country will decide what they want. I am a fahfee runner, that's my job. I work, I decide what kind of South Africa do I want. I write it down on a piece of paper and send it to this Congress where it becomes law. So what kind of South Africa do you want?

MAMARITI: I want to stay right here in my house. It's freehold. My husband bought it. Paid good money for it. It's my right.

FAHFEE: Ag Mama. Freehold is just the beginning. We want decent jobs, decent education, decent food, and decent life for all. (*He takes one of the potatoes* MAMARITI *has been peeling, throws it into the air and catches it.*) If we grow something, it's ours. If we make something, it's ours. So what's the magic number?

RUTH: 26.

FAHFEE: Hayikhona! Ten thousand in the Defiance Campaign. Do you remember the 1946 strikes, Mama?

MAMARITI: Ja.

FAHFEE: Forty thousand. Forty thousand miners in the ratholes, saying no. The Chinaman, he's got 36 numbers but I never win. But forty thousand, that's a number I can understand. Imagine a Softown strike! Fifty thousand! Then see if the Boere can move us. So, what else do you want, people?

RUTH: I'd like to find a way for Lulu to be in school.

LULU: I'm not going to school!

MAMARITI: I sell mbamba day and night to send you to school. Look at my hands. They're working for your future.

LULU: There is no future, Mama. Unless we make it. This education is rubbish.

MAMARITI: You must go to school – anything is better than nothing.

LULU: No, Mama. This is less than nothing. What do they

teach us? Nothing! Which natives live in which native reserve; education for certain forms of labour; whites originate in Africa; civilization comes from Europe; English only from Standard Six.

JAKES: English only from Standard Six? Now that's a terrible thing to do. If there was one thing we got from our church schools, it was a love of English.

LULU: Ja, they want us illiterate.

RUTH: Well you're not going to be illiterate if you can speak Zulu and Xhosa and Sotho.

JAKES: English is the language that unifies us.

RUTH: Okay. But you don't want to lose your own language.

JAKES: Look – you're Jewish, right?

RUTH: So?

JAKES: Well, can you speak Hebrew? Besides this Baruch Atah.

RUTH: No.

JAKES: But you're still Jewish, right?

RUTH: Look, I'm a South African first.

JAKES: And what does that mean?

RUTH: I'm a white, English-speaking South African.

JAKES: But you're still Jewish and you can't speak Hebrew, right? And that proves my point.

RUTH: Well, frankly I wish I could speak Hebrew. Jakes, I just think it's a terrible thing to lose a language. Imagine if I was the last person who could speak Hebrew? When I died, those words would be gone forever.

JAKES: You don't look so worried.

RUTH: I am worried.

JAKES: What's gone is gone. You can't hold on to the past.

These native reserves that Verwoerd wants, what have they got to do with Sophiatown? Here we listen to Bach and Beethoven. We listen to great American jazz. We read great Russian novels. We are a brand-new generation.

RUTH: Well, Lulu's not going to read anything if she doesn't go to school.

LULU: Even if I wanted to go to school, I can't. The school is going to be closed in April. Anyway, we'll be in Meadowlands.

FAHFEE: You must never say that, you hear! You give up before the fight!

RUTH: If you don't go to school, what are you gonna do?

LULU: We're going to make our own schools – under trees, in dance halls, in special culture clubs, in shebeens . . .

RUTH: In the shebeens?

JAKES: Yes – Mamariti's Special Shebeen School for Young Girls!

FAHFEE: Don't make jokes, Mr Drum.

LULU: It's not a joke. There are going to be schools in shebeens.

RUTH: And who is going to teach in these new schools?

LULU: I don't know. The teachers.

RUTH: Yes, that's the problem – new schools, Verwoerd's teachers.

FAHFEE: I'll teach her. Mathematics – dis my forte! I'm an expert on numbers. What's 49 times 49? Yes! Yes! Yes! Two thousand four hundred and one!

JAKES: How did you do that??

FAHFEE: I worked it out yesterday!

JAKES: I'll teach English literature . . . Africa's use of the short story.

RUTH: I'll teach English composition and biology. I was great in Biology at school.

54   Act 2

(*Enter* MINGUS.)

MINGUS: Charlie! Where the hell is he? What's going on here? Restaurant? Princess! Waar's daai tjerrie? I'll moer her! She's a rubberneck. Head this way! Head that way! This morning she's dressed up to kill – she won't even tell me where she's going.

(*Enter* CHARLIE.)

MINGUS: Charlie! Gaan vat daai Delilah and bring haar hierso. She's 'n rubberneck. Gaan! Speed!

(*Exit* CHARLIE.)

MINGUS: So? Sny my nou die mello. Cut me into the story. What's going on here?

FAHFEE: Listen, Mingus, we need the Americans' help. We're not going to move. Ons pola hier.

MINGUS: Niks. Politicians is one thing – Americans is another.

FAHFEE: Luister, Mingus, if we move from Sophia, these Americans, these Berliners, these Vultures are finished.

MINGUS: Never – we're not going!

FAHFEE: It's easy to talk – talk is cheap. We must organize. Remember the 1949 tram boycotts? The Berliners were there, man, fighting the police.

MINGUS: The Berliners were there, alright, but were they smart? No! One side only. In the tram boycott the Americans were smart, man. The Congress wants us to hit the tram users. So, early in the morning we move out. 'Hey – where you going? Don't you know it's boycott? The city wants to rob you man.' Kah! Kah! We hit them, man. And we get paid. Then at night the tram companies pay us to use the trams as if we're coming home from work – twice paid! That's what I call American style.

FAHFEE: You can't do that. It's one side or the other.

MINGUS: Money is money, Fahfee!

FAHFEE: Luister, Mingus. The G-men are always after you, right?

MINGUS: Right.

FAHFEE: Why?

MINGUS: Because we are the enemy man. They can't get us – we're too smart.

FAHFEE: Yes, but they're always after you.

MINGUS: Aah! Fokken spies! We'll get them. Just one day we'll get them.

FAHFEE: Mingus, have you ever been to Freedom Square? Seen the thousands of people there? Why are the G-men always coming with Sten guns to break up the meetings?

MINGUS: Why?

FAHFEE: Because the politicians are the enemy, man, just like the Americans, just like the Berliners.

MINGUS: Don't talk to me about the Berliners!

FAHFEE: Listen, you stupid Mingus. You and the Berliners, you fight each other – you should fight the real enemy.

MINGUS: The Berliners are the real enemy.

FAHFEE: We need you Mingus. We need the Americans to fight. We need the numbers, man. We need fighters. We need planners. We need the Berliners and the Americans and the Vultures and the school children, and the journalists to fight. Can't you see what's going on?

JAKES: What's going on? Hundreds of people living in shacks, paying rents so home-owners can get rich – that's what's going on. Nobody's going to stop them moving. They're going to get houses.

FAHFEE: Where? Twenty miles from town. So Verwoerd has a clean white city.

MINGUS: The trains, hey, easy pickings. An American's paradise.

FAHFEE: Sis, Mingus. The Boere are making a little thief out of you, robbing people on trains. This is history – we're in history and we're fighting for freedom.

MINGUS: Hey teacher, what is this history? They teach Lulu history in school. What does it help? I stole this, I stole that. Is that history?

JAKES: It's only history if you steal something really large – like a country. Then it's history.

FAHFEE: Ja, well, we're going to steal it back. And we start with Sophiatown. We must organize. What are the numbers? Seven to a street – with a leader. Seven leaders to a ward. Seven times seven. Forty nine. Forty-nine times forty-nine. The magic is in the numbers. We'll steal back our country with numbers.

(*Enter* CHARLIE *carrying* PRINCESS. *She is protesting wildly.*)

PRINCESS: Put me down! Put me down! You're a bloody stupid! Charlie, what are you doing? Put me down!

(*She is released and stands in the middle of the room. She is wearing a stunning but dishevelled outfit.*)

MINGUS: Ja – where have you been?

PRINCESS: What's it got to do with you?

(MINGUS *casually walks up to* PRINCESS *and then suddenly cracks her across the face.*)

MINGUS: Kom, jong, shoot die six, Princess. Sny my nou die mello. Cut me into the story.

PRINCESS: I've got a job.

MINGUS: What job?

PRINCESS: I've got a job as a model for a photographer.

MINGUS: Ja. And who's this photographer?

PRINCESS: He's from Holland.

MINGUS: Aah! A larnie Hollandse photographer! Come show me what you do.

Scene 1 57

PRINCESS: What you mean?

MINGUS: Show me!

PRINCESS: What?

MINGUS: How you do this modelling.

PRINCESS: Come on, Mingus.

MINGUS: Show!

(*She makes a half-hearted attempt to strike some poses.*)

MINGUS: You . . . you do that for this photographer?

PRINCESS: Yes.

MINGUS: Come on, take off this dress – it's mine!

PRINCESS: No, Mingus.

MINGUS: Com'on – I want to see how you look without my dresses.

(*He attempts to pull off her dress. She resists, then runs off screaming. He runs after her, shouting, followed by the others. Only* JAKES *and* RUTH *remain.*)

MINGUS: (*Running after* PRINCESS.) I want them all back. My dresses, the jewellery, die bloody lot. Come, let's see if you look like a princess then.

RUTH: I don't know why she doesn't leave.

JAKES: If I were you I'd stay right out of it. This is one thing you'll never understand.

RUTH: It's just plain bullying.

JAKES: She belongs to him, and that's that!

RUTH: Now that I don't understand.

JAKES: Look, to be frank – there is plenty that you'll never understand because you'll always be looking from the outside.

RUTH: In that case, I'm a lot like you. You're always looking from the outside, watching.

JAKES: Rubbish!

RUTH: Well, why don't you join Fahfee? He needs you. You can't watch for ever, you know.

JAKES: When I decide the time is right, I'll be a different person.

RUTH: I think you're just scared.

JAKES: Well, what about you?

RUTH: I'm here.

JAKES: You think that is enough? If you were a princess in Princess's position, what would you do?

RUTH: I'd fight. There's no question. Nobody treats me like that. I wouldn't tolerate it.

JAKES: Mingus would just fuck you up.

RUTH: Well, if I was treated like that, I would just leave.

JAKES: Where would you go? She's a princess from the slums – no name, no home, no family. She'll sleep wherever she can find a place. Now she's got a place – she'll stay. The truth is, no matter wherever you go, if something really happens to you, you'll just go home to Daddy or Uncle or just the whites – rich and warm and loving. It's just another kind of laager.

RUTH: Well, you're in your own kind of laager, aren't you Jakes? Buried in this new journalism, and the African short story. Why don't you get out for a while? Look at me. You write about me, but you never look at me properly. Try to see beyond your own fictions. It's me, Ruth Golden, the girl with the golden heart, pert, comfortable, curious. Why don't you look at me properly, Jakes. Just once?

(*Blackout.*)

Act 2   Scene 2

(*Spotlight on* RUTH. *She is concentrating intensely.*)

RUTH: 17, Diamond Lady; 18, Small Change; 19, Little Girl; 20, Cat; 21, Elephant; 22, Ship; 23, Long Hair; 24 Big Mouth; 25, Big House; 26, Bees.

(*Blackout.*)

Act 2   Scene 3

(*Enter the four men dressed in immaculate evening dress, white jackets, bowties, walking-sticks, and hats pulled low over the eyes. As they sing, they execute dance steps reminiscent of the Manhattan Brothers.*)

BANTU BAHLALA

Bantu bahlala ngenhliziy' ezibuhlungu
Sophia ngeyami (2)
Bantwana baydlala
Bazali bayakhala
Bakhalel' ilizwe labo
Sophia ngeyam' (2)

Sithi yebo yebo yebo yebo
Sophia ngeyami (2)
Nanka amabhunu
Afikile ngebulldoza
Adiliz' imizi yethu
Sophia ngeyam' (2)

(People stay with sad hearts
Sophiatown is mine (2)
Children are playing
Parents are weeping
Weeping for their land
Sophiatown is mine (2)

    We say yes, yes, yes, yes
    Sophiatown is mine
    Here come the Boers
    Coming with the bulldozer
    They destroy our homes
    Sophiatown is mine) (2)

(*Blackout.*)

Act 2   Scene 4

(*It is midnight. Enter* RUTH *in a nightdress, carrying a paraffin lamp. She sneaks up to the typewriter and begins to read one of* JAKES's *stories. Suddenly there is a noise behind her. Enter* MINGUS. *He is dressed to kill, hat brim pulled low, trench coat. He has returned from a job. He stands in the doorway.*)

MINGUS: What are you doing?

RUTH: Oh God, Mingus – you gave me a fright.

MINGUS: Come on Ruth Golden, what are you doing?

RUTH: I couldn't sleep.

MINGUS: Ja, and so you scratch in Jakes' things. What do you want?

RUTH: I'm just looking.

MINGUS: Why? What do you think you'll find there that you don't know already? Haven't you seen enough?

RUTH: Look, I couldn't sleep.

MINGUS: Why? Does Princess keep you awake, that you have to wander around at night?

RUTH: We manage.

MINGUS: Ja, and how does Sophiatown look now? Two in a bed – or does Princess sleep underneath?

RUTH: You kicked her out, and your mother wants the rent, so we manage.

MINGUS: Ja, and when the majietas come? One underneath and one on top! Sophiatown style.

RUTH: What do you want, Mingus?

MINGUS: From you, Miss Golden – nothing.

RUTH: Good, I'll just go right back to bed.

MINGUS: Hold it!

RUTH: What do you want, Mingus?

MINGUS: Come here! Come on. Give me your hand. I've just been on a job. Here – feel.

(*He puts her hand under his jacket.*)

RUTH: (*Pulling away.*) Ah.

MINGUS: Tonight there's no sleep for either of us. What I need now is a drive, a ride in the moonlight. I need to look at the moon.

RUTH: Why don't you go, Mingus?

MINGUS: Hold it. I want you to come with. It's lonely out there on your own. I want to look at your hair, your face, the rest of you.

RUTH: I'm tired. I'm going to bed.

MINGUS: (*Blocking her exit.*) If you want to see Sophiatown you gotta see all sides. This is Sophiatown by night.

RUTH: Look Mingus, it's late. I don't feel like going for a drive.

MINGUS: Don't make no fuss. Mingus will begin to think that you don't care for him and he'll wonder why. What's the problem with the white girl that she won't get in a car and come for a midnight ride? Or is there something about Mingus' face she doesn't like?

RUTH: Look Mingus, that's not true and you know it. I'm not dressed. Look at me!

MINGUS: That's what I'm doing.

RUTH: I can't go out like this.

MINGUS: Luister! Al die tjerries van Softown will come out with Mingus any time. But because you're too much of a larnie, you make yourself a can't-get, a nylon.

RUTH: Mingus, why are you making it so difficult for me? I'm living in Sophiatown, having a good time, and you're making it impossible.

MINGUS: You call this a good time? Julle larnies, julle is fokken mal. You come all the way from the white suburbs where it's all bloody fancy, and what is happening there? Niks. So you come here and Mingus is offering you a nice ride in the moonlight underneath the madness of the moon, and you say no.

RUTH: I just don't feel like it, okay?

MINGUS: Hey, what's the matter with you? What are you doing here anyway?

RUTH: Not what you think.

MINGUS: Luister, nobody says no to Mingus.

RUTH: Well, this person does!

(*Exit* RUTH. MINGUS *begins to follow her, then changes his mind. He makes for the exit, then turns back suddenly and shouts after her.*)

MINGUS: Hey! Nobody says no to Mingus, you skorrie morrie. You make promises with your eyes, and your bloody tits, shaking your bloody backside! And when the money's down you give nothing. How long do you think you can stay clean? Jou hoendervleis! You think I must lick your arse to get a ride with you? Jy's net 'n gemors. A weggooi! Kom hierso! Ek is moer se cock and you're hiding right underneath your bloody corset. You bloody nylons, you're all the same, man. You try and you try but once a nylon, always a nylon! Bloody bitch!

(*Blackout.*)

Act 2   Scene 5

(*Enter* JAKES, *dishevelled. He sits himself at his typewriter. He looks as if he's been up all night.*)

JAKES: (*Pounding away.*) The bastards, the tricky bastards! What kind of a brain do you have to have to think like this? God give me the right words!

MAMARITI: (*Offstage.*) Hey, Jakes, it's five o'clock in the morning. Hey, tula wena! I want to sleep. Tik-tik! Are you mad, man? Hey, you must find somewhere else to live if you want to work at five o'clock in the morning!

(*Enter* LULU, *wearing a nightdress.*)

LULU: What's going on?

MAMARITI: Hey Lulu, tell that madman from Drum to stop die geraas.

LULU: Jakes, it's five o'clock in the morning.

JAKES: You tell your mother I pay good rent. This is my bedroom. You see the chalkline on the floor?

LULU: So?

JAKES: Well, I work in my bedroom, so leave me alone!

MAMARITI: (*Offstage.*) Luister! You bloody keep quiet – or out!

JAKES: Jesus, Ma, you're like the Boere. You want me on the streets. I'm working, I pay rent, this is my space, pitiful as it is, and history is being made right now – and you want silence!

(*There is a knocking on the door.*)

JAKES: Jesus Christ! What now? Surely not today?

(*Enter* FAHFEE, *carrying a suitcase.*)

FAHFEE: They got me. They knocked down my shack before my eyes.

MINGUS: (*Offstage.*) Come on, come on – move these boxes! Charlie, you useless! You must move, man.

64   Act 2

(*Enter* MINGUS *and* CHARLIE. *They are in a panic. They're carrying piles of boxes. There is an immediate uproar.*)

MINGUS: Make space! Make space! We got work to do.

(*Enter* RUTH *in a nightdress.*)

RUTH: What's going on?

LULU: What's all these boxes?

JAKES: What's the story, Mingus?

MINGUS: Come help! Don't just stand there – move your arse! Get these boxes in – com'on. Hey, hoendervleis, kom help.

(*Exit* MINGUS, LULU, RUTH *and* CHARLIE *to carry more boxes. Enter* MAMARITI.)

MAMARITI: What's happening? It's five o'clock in the morning.

JAKES: Toby Street removals, Ma. Three days early.

MAMARITI: Jesus!

(*Exit* MAMARITI, *enter* MINGUS.)

MINGUS: Don't just stand there, Jakes, come and help.

JAKES: What's the story Mingus?

MINGUS: There's no story. Work for your living for a change! Have you ever done a stroke of honest work? No! Just sit down and tik-tik-tik all day. Kom, help.

JAKES: Com'on Mingus, what's the story?

MINGUS: Those bastard G-men knocked down my store-room in Toby Street. I've been like a rat all night – dodge here, dodge there! I'm everywhere!

(*Exit* MINGUS *for more boxes. Enter* MAMARITI, *dressed.*)

FAHFEE: Where you going, Ma?

MAMARITI: I'm going to see.

FAHFEE: No, Ma. There's trouble out there.

MAMARITI: Hey, wena, I'm going to see.

FAHFEE: You just stay right here.

MAMARITI: I'm going!

(*Exit* MAMARITI. *Enter* MINGUS *and* CHARLIE, *who move some boxes into* JAKES's *space.*)

JAKES: Hey Mingus, how long are these boxes going to be here? Where do I sleep?

MINGUS: You're lucky you've got a room at all. In fact, you're on one minute's notice. I'm sick and tired of you. Uit! You bloody situations, you're full of words. And what have they done? Have they saved my store-room in Toby Street?

FAHFEE: Ja, Mingus is right. Congress is always sending letters to City Council. It's rubbish. They just laugh and send an official apology. Words on paper – useless. It must be guns against guns. Then things will happen.

RUTH: (*Coming in carrying a box.*) What did happen, Mingus?

MINGUS: Ja, white girl. What do you do? You never work. You just want, want.

RUTH: What's going on, Jakes.

MINGUS: You're a bloody good-for-nothing! You whites, you're breaking down all our houses.

RUTH: I'm doing no such thing!

MINGUS: Well, who's doing it?

FAHFEE: They came three days early, like tricksters, conmen. They're loading people onto trucks and nobody's doing a thing. It's pitiful – families everywhere. They went for the leaders.

MINGUS: Ja, white girl – it's your fault!

RUTH: My fault? How can you say a bloody stupid thing like that?

MINGUS: What are you doing to stop them?

RUTH: What are you doing? Jakes, tell him to lay off.

(RUTH *finds protection behind* JAKES. MINGUS *moves in on her.*)

MINGUS: Don't cry to Jakes, it's your fathers and uncles and brothers who are doing this to us.

RUTH: My father has never hurt anybody in his life.

MINGUS: Don't talk to me like that. I'll cut you up. I'll kill you! I'll kill you!

FAHFEE: Luister, Mingus. This is only Ruth Golden. Choose your targets carefully. Daar's wit mense in Congress – baklei die Boere.

JAKES: Ja Mingus – what have you done to stop them?

MINGUS: I was working.

FAHFEE: Stealing.

MINGUS: That's my business. They steal from us – we steal from them.

FAHFEE: Ja, and how does it help?

JAKES: How does it help, Fahfee? Where's the M-plan? Where's the strike? Where are the gangs? How can I make a story out of this? The largest move in the history of the 1950s and nothing has happened.

FAHFEE: Some people have moved into the church to avoid the lorries.

JAKES: And you?

FAHFEE: I'm hiding – I need a place to sleep.

MINGUS: Sleep in the bath under the boxes!

(*Enter* PRINCESS, *immaculately dressed, carrying a suitcase.*)

PRINCESS: You can sleep in my place – I'm leaving.

MINGUS: Charlie! Let's get the hell out of this hole.

(*Exit* CHARLIE *and* MINGUS.)

PRINCESS: Ja, you can all stay here – in the rubble. I'm going to Hillbrow. Nobody's going to catch me like a fool in Meadowlands. Princess is Number One. I've got a flat. I've got a man with manners. I got perfume – and chocolate. I'm going. This Softown, it's finished.

(*Silence. They all look at her. She exits.*)

(*Fade to black.*)

Act 2   Scene 6

(MINGUS *is tying up his stolen goods and possessions. On centre stage, ropes and boxes abound.* CHARLIE *and* MINGUS *attempt to make some order.*)

MINGUS: Come on, Charlie, we gotta load all these things on the G.G.'s truck. Looks like junk doesn't it, Charlie, but we know it's not. Come on, what's in that box? Jewellery! from Katz en Lourie. And that box? No, no, no – you gotta handle it with utmost care. Gently. Put it down. Turn it over now. And do you know what's in that box? Stetson hats. When I get down to Meadowlands, I'll be selling them there. I hear say these trains from Meadowlands are going to be easy pickings, and if the fences keep us in, they'll keep the G-men out – you'll see.

Do you know what's in that box? I thought as much. You don't know a damn thing – all your life you're depending on this brain, living on this man, and what have you learnt? Nothing. Just dumb hands for carrying and dumb legs for running behind my tail.

(*Exit* CHARLIE.)

Well, four rooms in Meadowlands doesn't seem such a bad prospect.

(*Enter* CHARLIE *with a small tattered suitcase.*)

MINGUS: Hey hey hey! What do you think you're doing? Where you putting that suitcase of yours?

CHARLIE: I'm going to get a house.

MINGUS: (*Laughing*.) One thing is very clear – that suitcase does not belong to me, Charlie, so the best thing for you to do is move it right away.

CHARLIE: I'll get a house!

MINGUS: Come on Charlie, you'll get a labour camp! I think I'm right in presuming that it is only my assets and properties that are going with me to Meadowlands. So I think the best thing for you to do is to get your suitcase well away!

CHARLIE: No!

MINGUS: What you mean, Charlie? The time has come for you to go your way and I get going my way.

CHARLIE: No!

MINGUS: Look, Charlie, for your own good – just move your stuff away.

CHARLIE: No! I'm going with you.

MINGUS: Just move it away!

CHARLIE: No! I can't stay here. What will I do? Everything I've done for you.

MINGUS: I'm not going anywhere with you. Now get that into your head. I can't keep watching for you all your life. It's the end! So just move your things away. I'm going to live in Meadowlands. There's no place for you there. So just leave me be.

CHARLIE: Ons dak nie. Ons pola hier.

MINGUS: Are you kidding? We've already lost. We'll stay wherever they want us to.

CHARLIE: So you want to leave me here to die! You're just going to dump me. I'm not staying here. I'm coming with you.

MINGUS: Now, Charlie – be a man!

CHARLIE: I am a man! Where must I sleep? In the rubble?

Where will I live? Where are the old cars? Where are the tin shacks? Where are all the houses?

MINGUS: Charlie! I didn't know you had so many words in you! I'm amazed!

CHARLIE: (*Immediately at a loss.*) I'm Charlie . . .

MINGUS: Now Charlie, relax. Look, I've got a plan. Now listen. When I get to the house, I'll send a driver back to come and pick you up – with your suitcase – in style.

CHARLIE: No, man!

MINGUS: Look, we're gonna have a full truck but I'll get someone to fetch you. Now sit, Charlie, take your suitcase and sit. I'll be back in a minute.

CHARLIE: You're lying to me! You'll never come back.

MINGUS: I will.

CHARLIE: No you won't. Don't try and stop me.

MINGUS: Alright! Now just do yourself a worldly favour . . . .

CHARLIE: No no no. Don't try and talk to me. You just want to dump me.

MINGUS: Will you listen! If you listen I'll explain.

CHARLIE: No!

MINGUS: (*With uncharacteristic compassion.*) Charlie, do you know who you are? Have you ever looked at yourself, stared at that face of yours, and asked yourself who you are? Looked in the car mirror and asked, 'Who am I?' You just can't come with me.

CHARLIE: I will!

MINGUS: No! Listen. You can't come with me because you're a Coloured. Me – I'm a black, black as the ace of spades. But you're Coloured. Me, I'm going to Meadowlands because we lost, but you can't. Just understand one thing, Charlie. We lost Sophiatown and you're on your own. So just take your suitcase and say goodbye. Please, Charlie, goodbye.

(CHARLIE *and* MINGUS *freeze in their positions of parting on opposite sides of the stage.* RUTH *enters from one side,* JAKES *from the other.* RUTH *is carrying all her suitcases.*)

RUTH: So this is it.

JAKES: This is it.

RUTH: I can't stay here, I know that. And I can't come with. So this is the end. I've come to say goodbye.

JAKES: (*Curtly.*) Goodbye.

RUTH: What's the matter with you, Jakes? I've been waiting for weeks for you to show me a sign, one sign of real interest.

JAKES: Ja.

RUTH: You won't let me reach you. You're like a brick wall. What do you want me to do?

JAKES: There's nothing you can do.

RUTH: If you had opened up for a moment, anything would have been possible.

JAKES: It isn't possible, because I've decided that it isn't possible. I'm not letting some white girl put her hands around my heart when she feels like it. You want to ride me over like a bulldozer and leave me here for dust. But I'm not going to allow it. We lost what little chance we had.

RUTH: We never took it.

JAKES: Well, let's just say we failed. We let the Boere drive a wedge between us. Who gives a damn whether a black journalist and a white storyteller can or can't meet? When the war comes, as it will, it will be fought in the barren ground between us, and it will be so large as to make us invisible.

RUTH: I'm not talking about a war. I'm talking about us.

JAKES: We can't begin to talk about us – not until this war has been fought and won.

RUTH: There are other countries.

JAKES: There's nowhere to go, except Yeoville and Meadowlands. No matter where we run, these places will always haunt us. Ruth in Yeoville, Jakes in Meadowlands. Truth is, all the time you've been with us, we've both known you have a back door to Yeoville.

RUTH: That door is closed, Jakes.

JAKES: No, it's not.

RUTH: Yes, it is.

JAKES: Nonsense.

RUTH: Jakes. Right now I don't know where I'm going, but the door to Yeoville is shut.

JAKES: No . . .

RUTH: I'm the one who's closing it.

(*Lights change.*)

Act 2   Scene 7

(*The Cast sing 'Boph' umthwalo' as they enter.*)

> Boph' umthwalo
> sigoduke (4)
>
> Siya' shiya
> iKofifi (4)
>
> (We pack up and we leave (4)
> We're leaving Sophiatown) (4)

(*As the Cast sing, they slowly place a lifetime's furniture and possessions in a pile around* JAKES's *desk. The old bath is carefully laid on its side.* MAMARITI *climbs onto her chair which has been placed on top of an old tin trunk. The other members of the Cast each take up a special position and recite their monologues over the singing. The stage becomes very quiet, only the hum of the song remaining. The lighting is moody. Faces are picked out by spotlights.*)

72 Act 2

MAMARITI: The day they moved us out, it was the day the big rains fell. That was the day of the tears and the day of the Saracens.

LULU: We watched them move the first street, Toby Street, where Dr Xuma was. The rain was falling and we were only a few. The bulldozers were there knocking down the pillars of the first house. I don't remember the name of the people. That was Toby Street where Dr Xuma was – right next to Westdene. Father Huddleston, Dr Xuma, Bo Resha and Oliver Tambo were there.

MINGUS: The bulldozers bulldozed five houses: one, two, three, four, five at the same time. As they were bulldozing the houses, the lorries that were supplied by the G.G. were taking the loads out to Meadowlands.

MAMARITI: The day my house was removed, it was half-past five in the morning. I think it was on a Thursday. They knocked at my door. Three loud knocks. Five tall Dutchmen. They said the day had come. I wished for a special sign on my door, but there was none.

LULU: The lorries were waiting. Even as we packed, the labourers with the Boere were hitting the pillars of the verandah with big hammers.

MAMARITI: I said to them, I wished they could give us enough time to pack, as I was going to have my cups and my plates broken.

LULU: And they said, 'Jy praat te veel. Moenie praat nie.' And Ma said, 'I have the right to talk for my things.' By eight o'clock we were already moved to Meadowlands. The walls and the floors of the house were rough cement. Everything was awful and we were very much unhappy.

MAMARITI: I was sitting on my chair on the lorry and I started shouting, 'I'm not getting down! I'm not going to stay in that Meadowlands house. I'm afraid. Take off the load from the lorry but I'm not getting down. I'd rather die. Dump me anywhere, I'd rather die!'

(*The Cast complete the song.*)

FAHFEE: These Boere, they are very tricky. Three days early they came, and we weren't prepared. There were two thousand G-men lining the streets. Everywhere, there were slogans on the walls: 'We won't move.' 'This is home.' 'Hands off Sophiatown.' But what could we do against eighty lorries and two thousand police? We tried to organize a general stayaway. At three o'clock the following Monday morning we ran through the streets hitting the telegraph poles with iron bars. Wake up!

(CHARLIE *strikes one of the telegraph poles with an iron bar. Sharp lighting change.*)

Vukani! (CHARLIE *hits the pole.*) Strike! (*Hits.*) General stayaway! (*Hits.*) I remember the last time they hit the telegraph poles it was before the 1950 riots. The Youth League. They wanted real violence and the Berliners were ready, but Congress said no.

Stone the street lamps! (*Hits.*) Let the Gatas move in the dark. (*Hits.*) Watch out! (*Hits.*) Watch out! (*Hits.*) Watch out! The Gatas are coming! These Berliners! These Americans! They could fight. (*Hits.*) Pole against street lamp. (*Hits.*) Bar against telegraph pole. But the time was not right. The Gatas did their job, and the buses left for work as usual.

I signal Bees. If this number comes up – 26 – we signal Bees. Bees mean trouble, large crowds, army. Well, I signal Bees. Ja, I signal Bees. They can't stop us forever.

(*The Cast resume the song as they regroup on the stage to resemble a family portrait.* JAKES *rises to speak.*)

JAKES: This bitterness inside me wells up and chokes. We lost, and Sophiatown is rubble. The visions of the mad Boere smashed this hope, turned it to rubble. And out of this dust, like a carefully planned joke, Triomf rises. What triumph is this? Triumph over music? Triumph over meeting? Triumph over the future? Sophiatown was a cancer on a pure white city, moved out at gunpoint by madmen. With its going, the last common ground is gone. The war has been declared, the battle sides are drawn. Yeoville and Meadowlands, and a wasteland in-between.

I don't want to die like Can Themba, of alcohol poisoning, in a country that is not my own. I don't want the streets of New York to take me, as they did Nat Nakasa. The streets of New York broke his bones, but South Africa broke his spirit.

Exile – an interminable death. It eats out the very centre of your heart. Arthur Maimane, Todd Matshikiza, Bloke Modisane, Lewis Nkosi, Hugh Masekela, Dollar Brand, Miriam Makeba, Jonas Gwangwa – all our best and brightest driven out by this Triomf.

And 65 Gerty Street? Princess and her Dutch lover escaped the Immorality Act by going to Europe. Lulu is without education. The G-men, they caught up with Mingus, and he served time in Number Four. Coming out, he was a qualified plumber. Mama died of a broken heart. Fahfee disappeared. Some say he was recruited – joined Umkhonto We Sizwe.

Ruth we never see. We tried for a while but meeting seemed impossible.

Oh yes – Charlie . . . Charlie we found stabbed to death in the bricks and rubble at the old house. He was living in a pipe and got into a fight. Some say he crawled five blocks to get to Gerty Street. His body was found lying in the brick and the rubble over the upturned bath.

This destruction is called Triomf. I hope the dust of that triumph settles deep in the lungs like a disease and covers these purified suburbs with ash. Memory is a weapon. Only a long rain will clean away these tears.

(*The Cast sing 'Izinyembezi zabantu'.*)

IZINYEMBEZI ZABANTU

Izinyembezi zabantu (3)
Sophiatown, Sophiatown, Sophiatown
Izinyembezi zabantu

Kwadum' izulu, lana
Kwanyakaz' umhlaba
Siyakushiya Sophiatown (2)
Izinyembezi zabantu

Sibona, kughamuk' amaphoyisa
Kudum' ibulldoza
Kwaghamuk' umntwana
Kwaphuma bonk' omakhelwana
Siyakushiya Sophiatown (2)

Izinyembezi zabantu (3)

(Tears of the people (3)
Sophiatown, Sophiatown, Sophiatown
Tears of the people

It thunders, it rains
The earth trembles
We are leaving you, Sophiatown (2)
Tears of the people

We see the police appearing
The bulldozer thunders
A child jumps out
All the neighbours appear
We are leaving you, Sophiatown (2)

Tears of the people) (3)

(*Fade to black.*)

FINIS

Glossary

ACT 1 SCENE 1

Kofifi – Sophiatown
moegoes – greenhorns
voetsak – bugger off
G-men – government men, i.e. policemen
wietie – to talk, chat
wiebits – girls
mataras – women
majietas – young men
'n bla van 'n man – a buddy
skryf – write
'n situation – an intellectual
'n outie – a gangster
gonee – knife
jungle – knife
Boere – Boers, Afrikaners
Dikgang tsa gompieno – News of the Day
ousie – girl, chick
ouens – guys

ACT 1 SCENE 2

skelm – thief
slegte vrou – bad woman
tjerrie – girl
dis khuvet onder die korset – it's all fine
hoozit? – how's it?
plek – place

ACT 1 SCENE 3

ek mnca jou – I crave you
bioscope – cinema
klap – slap
Hai! Wena ungakhulumi umswanila nxa – Hey, you stop talking tripe here!

ACT 1 SCENE 4

This scene is mostly written in Tsotsitaal.
die matara van die dla – the lady of the house
jy's mooi – you're pretty
moenie baaiza nie – don't put a foot wrong
die magrizin van die stuk – the mistress of the house
nylon – well-bred girl

torch daai wiebit – look at that chick
ek hak jou – I like you
to Katz en Lourie – to marry
trou – marry
dis singalie – it's grand
Maklera – Newclare
moemishes – bumpkins, fools
jy notch? – do you get it?
zetz – slap
larnie – white person
hayikhona – no
taal – language

ACT 1   SCENE 6

klerrie – clear out
ons dak nie – we're not moving

ACT 1   SCENE 7

madlozis – ancestors
rappe – watches

ACT 2   SCENE 1

gee pad – give way
mbamba – home-brewed beer
ba tla bona marago a noga – They'll see the backside of a snake
I'll moer her – I'll fuck her up
sny my nou die mello – fill me in with the story
shoot die six – cut me into the story

ACT 2   SCENE 4

skorrie morrie – good for nothing
hoendervleis – chicken girl (chicken flesh)
jy's net 'n gemors – you're just a piece of trash
weggooi – a piece of rubbish

ACT 2   SCENE 5

tula wena – be quiet
geraas – noise
daars wit mense in die Congress – there are white people in the Congress
baklei – fight

ACT 2   SCENE 7

jy praat te veel – you're talking too much

Sophiatown

"A glorious celebration" — *Weekly Mail*

"Invigorating and uplifting" — *The Star Tonight*

"Sheer joy" — *Financial Times*

"Sophiatown . . . disciplined, radical and vigorously entertaining — *The List*, Glasgow

"Sophiatown is riveting" — *New Statesman*, London

"Unbearably poignant" — *The Guardian*, Manchester

"Sophiatown is a triumph" — *The Argus*

". . . a certain robust spirit of defiance and fulfilled living. . . . the sheer joy of it all is contagious" — *The Sowetan*

". . . a swing and a sensitivity to move the heart" — *Le Monde*, Paris